INSIGHT

CREATIVE SYSTEMS THEORY'S
RADICAL NEW PICTURE OF
HUMAN POSSIBILITY

CHARLES M. JOHNSTON, MD

The Institute for Creative Development (ICD) Press
Seattle, Washington

Publisher's Cataloging-In-Publication Data

Names: Johnston, Charles M., author.

Title: Insight: Creative Systems Theory's Radical New Picture of Human Possibility / Charles M. Johnston, MD.

Description: Seattle, Washington : The Institute for Creative Development (ICD) Press, [2022] | Includes bibliographical references and index.

Identifiers: ISBN 9781734243130 (print) | ISBN 9781734243154 (ebook)

Subjects: LCSH: Social evolution. | Social systems. | Civilization, Modern—Psychological aspects. | Conduct of life. | Future, The—Psychological aspects. | Johnston, Charles M.—Philosophy.

Classification: LCC HM626 .J644 2021 (print) | LCC HM626 (ebook) | DDC 303.4—dc23

The Institute for Creative Development (ICD) Press, Seattle, Washington

Cover design by Tahiratun Nesa Suborna

Author photo by Brad Kevelin

ISBN: 978-1-7342431-3-0

Library of Congress Control Number: 2021924703   First printing 2022

INSIGHT

Surprises...and More Surprises

Creative Systems Theory brings big-picture, long-term perspective to the human endeavor. And the theory's concept of Cultural Maturity specifically addresses the times we live in and the tasks ahead for the species. Together they offer an overarching framework that provides essential guidance for our times not found in other places. Each notion is radically new both in where it takes us and in the kind of thinking it represents.

The focus of this book is less the particulars of these ideas than this radical newness. While notions within Creative Systems Theory often have important historical antecedents and other people have asked related questions, the theory's most basic assumptions require that we understand in new ways. We can't get to them just by thinking harder or building on familiar beliefs. Ultimately where they take us makes a wholly new kind of contribution.

I've pointed toward this newness in previous writings, but until now I've not put it forefront. The reason in part is that I have not before been comfortable doing so. Such claims can too easily come across only as arrogance. And we live in times in which grand proclamations have become all too common. It is also the case that I have come to fully appreciate that newness only over time. I recognized a larger importance abstractly with these notions' beginnings some fifty years ago. But it has taken the course of my life for that more encompassing significance to be something that I could grasp in any complete way and articulate with confidence. The fundamental newness of these notions has been a continual teacher.

The concept of Cultural Maturity describes how human advancement will require a fundamentally new chapter in how we understand and act, an essential "growing up" as a species. And Creative Systems Theory's application of a creative frame brings a depth and nuance to our thinking that becomes possible only with this critical developmental step. Today I better understand the essential role that these notions' newness plays in their contribution to what our times require of us. I also more fully grasp how it is only in recognizing these notions' full importance—their significance in the larger story of ideas—that they can be deeply engaged and successfully applied. I now have no trouble voicing how it is that they make claims that people may initially find audacious. And I better recognize the importance of doing so.

Through the years, I've drawn on Creative Systems Theory and the concept of Cultural Maturity in multiple ways. Over decades with the Institute for Creative Development, a Seattle-based think tank and center for advanced leadership training, I worked to teach about and foster culturally mature leadership. And I and colleagues have applied Creative Systems Theory ideas to essential concerns that lie ahead for the species—from the future challenges of governance and government to what love and human relationship more generally will require of us. I've also written over a dozen books and numerous articles that in various ways expand on the ideas of Creative Systems Theory and the broader implications of culturally mature understanding.

Most often with my writing I've simply attempted to communicate ideas as clearly as I am able. Sometimes this has taken the form of short introductory volumes such as *Hope and the Future: Confronting Today's Crisis of Purpose*.[1] Often it has been with considerable detail as with my two overarching books—*Creative Systems Theory: A Comprehensive Theory of Purpose, Change, and Interrelationship in Human Systems*[2]

---

1 Charles M. Johnston, MD, *Hope and the Future: Confronting Today's Crisis of Purpose*, ICD Press, 2018.

2 Charles M. Johnston, MD, *Creative Systems Theory: A Comprehensive Theory of Purpose, Change, and Interrelationship in Human Systems*, ICD Press, 2021.

and *Cultural Maturity: A Guidebook for the Future.*[3] In these works I've sometimes noted larger, more philosophical/paradigmatic implications, but my primary purpose has been to help people grasp what for most are unfamiliar ideas and successfully put them into practice.

In other contexts, for example with my YouTube channel "Ask the Cultural Psychiatrist," I have taken a quite different approach. I've focused on how conclusions that follow from Cultural Maturity's needed new chapter in how we think and act are in the end straightforward— how when we are ready for them, they can seem like "common sense." In part I have used this approach simply because this observation is accurate—and can be extremely helpful. Because Cultural Maturity is a developmental notion, when culturally mature conclusions are timely, they can become almost obvious. I've also done so in order to encourage people to be open to essential ideas that on first encounter can easily overwhelm and confuse.

My approach with this short book is different yet. As important as these notion's details and their ultimately common-sense nature is the leap in understanding that they represent. Our task here will be to make sense of that leap and how Creative Systems Theory's success at making it results in thinking that is fundamentally new—and radical. We will examine how the changes that produce culturally mature understanding involve not just thinking new things—being smarter or more clever— but a new kind of cognitive organization. We will also examine how this cognitive reordering expands the way we think in ways that challenge past assumptions of every sort—from our beliefs about intelligence and human purpose to common assumptions about morality, freedom, or success. In the end, the leap in understanding that this cognitive reordering makes possible requires us to reexamine our most basic ideas about what makes us who we are and what constitutes truth.

The book will also fill out my claim that this leap, besides being radical in its newness, is also radically important. We will look at how it is essential not just to needed new ways of understanding but to addressing the most practical of concerns. I will go so far as to propose that if the picture presented by the concept of Cultural Maturity is not

---

3 Charles M. Johnston, MD, *Cultural Maturity: A Guidebook for the Future,* ICD Press, 2015.

basically correct, it is hard to be legitimately optimistic about our human future. I will also describe how Creative Systems Theory's broader conceptual framework, along with providing essential evidence that the concept of Cultural Maturity is correct, makes possible a dynamism and completeness to how we think and act that has not before been an option. I will argue that new kinds of conceptual tools like those provided by Creative Systems Theory will be essential if we are to effectively make our way—at least with any elegance.

The observation that the assumptions of the Modern Age are ultimately insufficient is not new. It has been made by many people—and not just recently, but over centuries. And the recognition that something at least similar to the leap I'm describing might be important is also not original to me. In footnotes I will cite a handful of thinkers whose work at least begins to engage the threshold of culturally mature understanding. But while some of these ideas have engaged that threshold, most have stopped well short. Creative Systems Theory's original contributions lie in the perspective it brings to understanding just what the leap that is required by our times involves and in how far the theory's ideas are able to take us into Cultural Maturity's new territory of experience.[4]

Some Background and Current Circumstances

Creative Systems Theory and the concept of Cultural Maturity did not have their start with interest in grand encompassing theory or some pressing desire on my part to solve major world problems. Early on in my life I found particular meaning in things creative. I was a sculptor and also a musician. In time, I found myself fascinated by creative process itself, by how it was that new possibility came into being. In my book *Creative Systems Theory*, I tell the story of how early reflections about the workings of formative process and intelligence's role in it evolved over time into the theory's overarching formulations.

---

4 With a few exceptions that I will note, my familiarity with the ideas of figures I cite came well after Creative Systems Theory's early development and initial articulation. Where they have benefited my thinking, it has been primarily in providing historical perspective and also in functioning like polishing stones against which to sharpen observations over the course of my life.

It has been a journey of continual surprises. Often the insights that I will touch on in the chapters ahead relate to questions that I had not before even thought to ask, and frequently what I discovered directly challenged what I had thought to be true. Topics that I highlight will span from the most personal levels of experience to observations about understanding at its most basic and existence as a whole. Many of the concerns that I will give attention to in the book could at first seem to have almost nothing to do with one another. But as we will see, the fundamental newness reflected in these observations ultimately comes from the same source.

My use of the word "leap" is not just metaphorical. Drawing on parallels from previous historical times helps put the audaciousness I suggest in high relief and also makes it more understandable. I will propose that the cognitive reordering that produces Cultural Maturity's changes reflects a leap in understanding for our time in the same sense that the new perspectives offered by the thinking of René Descartes or Sir Isaac Newton did in theirs—then with the leap that gave us Renaissance art, the Reformation, and eventually the Scientific Age and the possibility of modern representative government. And the audaciousness doesn't stop there. I will argue that there are important ways in which the significance of today's leap as articulated by the concept of Cultural Maturity is greater, and not just because it is pertinent to now—though certainly there is that. The cognitive reordering that produces culturally mature perspective offers that we might step back and grasp a more ultimately encompassing picture, one that helps us understand not just the tasks of our time, but also how it was that Descartes and Newton might have reached the particular conclusions that they did in theirs. In a similar way, it helps us better understand even earlier major change points in culture's story.

I have not always experienced the radical newness of these notions as a gift. Certainly it has often made my task in communicating about them more difficult. Often I've come up against obstacles that only came to make full sense years later. For example, I was sure early on in trying to write about the concept of Cultural Maturity that I had devised a simple way to do so. Cultural Maturity's changes make possible new kinds of human capacities, abilities that will be needed if we are to address the important questions before us. I assumed that simply describing those new capacities would provide an easily accessible way for people to grasp the concept of Cultural Maturity and its importance. But I kept hitting my head against a wall. I'd think I could write something in a few words, but I would end up going on for many pages and still not be satisfied. I had not recognized the Catch-22 inherent in my efforts. It turns out that understanding culturally mature capacities at all deeply itself requires culturally mature capacities.

This radical newness also meant that I sometimes had to let go not just of familiar beliefs, but of personally cherished beliefs. For example, when writing about how Creative Systems Theory addresses personality differences in my first book, I was confronted by a recognition that stopped me in my tracks. I saw that the whole of the book to that point reflected a bias toward the assumptions of my own personality style. I also realized that the consequences were more basic—and more of a deal-breaker as far as what the book's ideas were ultimately about— than just that notions might be biased in a particular direction. The concept of Cultural Maturity highlights how mature understanding requires drawing on the whole of cognition's systemic complexity. And the Creative Systems Personality Typology delineates how different temperaments draw preferentially on different aspects of that complexity. Without recognizing it, I was making the parts of that complexity that I was most familiar with the center of truth. In the process I was undermining exactly what I was attempting to accomplish. People who natively see the world through similar eyes might have found what I wrote insightful—or even wise (and having a ready audience, I would have sold more books). But I would ultimately have defeated my whole purpose. Because that error was reflected not just in specific content, but in my overall approach to writing, I had to, in effect, start over.

One consequence of the foundational nature of the leap that Creative Systems Theory and the concept of Cultural Maturity represents is that I have often needed to be more of a Lone Ranger in my efforts than I would have preferred. And this has often become more the case as I have come to better appreciate the significance of ideas, have more effectively articulated them, and have been more able to parse out differences from other contributions.

Responses to a couple of recent books have again reminded me of the depth of the challenge we face with Cultural Maturity's task. In an effort to reach a broader audience, I focused these books not so much on big-picture understanding than on issues currently in the news. *Perspective and Guidance for a Time of Deep Discord* confronts today's increasingly troubling degree of social and political polarization.[5] And *On the Evolution of Intimacy* addresses changes reshaping love and gender.[6] I wrote these books primarily because these topics are important. But I also wrote them because a good number of people today recognize that importance.

Each book has been well received. But with each I have had to face the fact that few people are yet ready to engage these topics with the complexity that they ultimately require. While many people do indeed consider polarization to be a problem, most assume that the difficulty lies with other people's polarized responses. (They fail to recognize that the problem is polarization itself—and to see the sense in which they themselves are complicit). Similarly, few people today who hold opinions about gender and identity are really interested in getting beyond simple-answer ideological interpretations. I'm often asked what percentage of the population I believe to be capable of well-developed culturally mature capacities. My best guess is something like 5 percent in the modern West. In spite of the front-page-news nature of these two books, the number of people who were able to recognize their importance and make full use of them was likely, again, around that 5 percent.

I should mention an additional dynamic that today further complicates understanding. In *Perspective and Guidance for a Time of Deep Discord*, I describe how we have seen regression with regard to Cultural Maturity's task over the last thirty years. This is easiest to recognize with the way people today are immediately taking sides with questions of all sorts—and often with regard to concerns where initially there were no obvious ideological positions. Rather than getting beyond the ideological, simple-answer thinking of times past, too often of late we have only retreated further into it. With many issues where it appeared we were making headway, instead today we see backsliding.

5   Charles M. Johnston, MD, *Perspective and Guidance for a Time of Deep Discord: Why We See Such Extreme Social and Political Polarization—and What We Can Do About It*, ICD Press, 2021.

6   Charles M. Johnston, MD, *On the Evolution of Intimacy: A Brief Exploration into the Past, Present, and Future of Gender and Love*, ICD Press, 2019.

Just why we encounter this backsliding remains an open question.[7] But I think it is reasonable to conclude that it could be twenty, thirty, or fifty years before the importance of the kinds of changes that the concept of Cultural Maturity points toward are widely appreciated, and well into the next century before we know whether we will be successful in addressing those changes. I've had to come to grips with the fact that much in these notions will likely not be graspable by any kind of a broad audience until well after I am gone. Accepting that fact has been important to my willingness to proceed with the work and to keeping my relationship with the work honest and creative.

A Layered Significance

Some of the more general aspects of what makes Creative Systems Theory ideas significant can, at least on first blush, seem not so much unique as simply unusual. For example, there is how the theory's ideas bring long-term perspective to essential questions. Creative Systems Theory's vantage looks out over decades, centuries, and more. We are more used to thinking in terms of more immediate concerns—if not of the front-page-news sort, then at least specific concerns of our time. There is also how Creative Systems Theory's vantage spans widely across realms of understanding. Truly interdisciplinary thinking remains rare.

But it turns out that even when it comes to these basic sorts of characteristics, we are dealing with fundamental newness. Most long-term historical thinking focuses on invention and possibility in the technical sense. Creative Systems Theory's specifically evolutionary sort of systemic vantage puts special emphasis on how the ways we think change over time, and in particular how they are changing in ours. Evolutionary thinking is not unique to Creative Systems Theory, but the particular kind of perspective that comes from the application of a creative frame is specifically new. I will describe how thinking of history in terms of chapters and epochs can be controversial, and for legitimate reasons. I will also make clear how the result with the application of creative a frame is evolutionary thinking that effectively gets beyond past objections.[8]

---

7 I will reflect on it in Chapter Five.

8 In many academic circles, ideas that view culture as evolving can be dis-

In a similar way, the theory emphasizes how understanding that spans domains today requires not just thinking that better makes connections, but wholly new, more dynamic and systemic ways of making sense of how connections work. Again, systemic understanding is not new. But because most systemic thinking remains mechanistic, it continues to leave us short of what such understanding ultimately needs to accomplish. I will describe how Creative Systems Theory's approach, in a whole new sense, allows us to think about systems in ways that reflect the fact that we are alive—and human.[9]

The foundation of Creative Systems Theory's unique contribution is the creative reframing that provides the basis for its formulations. Modern Age thought, at least of the more theoretical sort, has been rooted in the assumption that truth means rationally conceived, "objective" truth. With the cognitive reordering that produces culturally mature understanding, we better appreciate both how it is that intelligence has multiple aspects and also how objectivity as we have thought of it stops short of being complete. We also see how Modern Age understanding represents but one chapter in a larger story. The theory invites us to entertain a new, more specifically "creative"[10] kind of Fundamental Organizing Concept.

Creative Systems Theory addresses how our multiple intelligences work together to make us the toolmaking, meaning-making—we could say simply, creative—creatures that we are. And it delineates how, when we draw consciously on the whole of intelligence's creative

---

missed out of hand as "historicism." The most commonly cited reason for such dismissal is that evolutionary views have been used in times past to support racist interpretations and to justify the colonial enterprise. Reference is often made to Georg Hegel's philosophically idealist notions that postulated an ultimate Prussian state (and proved valuable to the Nazis). We can also find objection from people of postmodern persuasion who find any kind of overarching conception questionable. In later chapters I will examine how, while wariness is justified, such dismissing results in throwing out thinking that in fact will be increasingly critical to making our way. I will also propose that the reasons for dismissing such ideas tend to be deeper than those who do the dismissing tend to recognize.

9 See Chapter Three.

10 I will put the word "creative" in quotes when it feels important to emphasize that I am using the term in an unusually encompassing way.

complexity—as we do with Cultural Maturity's cognitive changes—it becomes possible to think with a dynamism and systemic completeness that has not before been an option. It also argues that this kind of greater completeness of understanding will be essential to any kind of future we would want to live in. The theory's radical claims each follow from this greater completeness.

An important related way that Creative Systems Theory's particular approach is new concerns how it views understanding's task. The theory's concern is not with truth in some absolutist sense, but rather with what appears to be true as a product of the perspective we bring to understanding (including the particular perspective that produces what we think of as objectivity in modern times). In the end, Creative Systems Theory is less about what we think than how we think. It is about human cognition and the different ways that human cognition organizes at different times and places. And in particular it is about how the leap in cognitive organization that defines today's developmental/creative imperative reorders understanding.

Where We Will Give Our Attention

The book's intended audience is different from that of my previous books. I am not so much interested in reaching a broad readership than with providing perspective for those who have particular interest in what makes the theory new and important. My purpose with this book will be to help clarify the leap that Creative Systems Theory proposes all effective thinking in times ahead must somehow succeed at making. And it is to make understandable both why that leap is critically important and the multiple ways that it manifests in the theory's diverse contributions. For people who might write about these notions after I am gone, it will help bring focus to the distinctions that define that significance.

Chapter One provides a brief introduction to Creative Systems Theory and the concept of Cultural Maturity. The chapters that follow each take on one particular kind of radical claim. With each, I will articulate that claim as clearly as I am able. I will also contrast that claim's conclusions with how we have thought about the topic it addresses in times past and also highlight some of its implications for the future.

Chapter Two brings focus to how culturally mature understanding reflects not just a next chapter in the human story, but a new kind of story. It delineates how more familiar ways of understanding the tasks ahead for the species—and ideological beliefs more generally—ultimately fail us. And it examines how the concept of Cultural Maturity provides needed guidance going forward. It also makes the radical proposal that culturally mature understanding reflects not just the kind of understanding needed for today, but what will be required of us well into humanity's future.

Chapter Three addresses the needed leap more conceptually and also how Creative Systems Theory succeeds at making it. It clarifies how the Modern Age assumption that reality is, in effect, a great machine ultimately proves insufficient (and also how the opposing arguments of romanticism and philosophical idealism get us no closer). And it examines how Creative Systems Theory's new Fundamental Organizing Concept—the idea that we can think of human cognitive processes as creatively ordered—lets us think in ways that better reflect that we are alive, and alive in the particular sense that makes us human. The chapter goes on to observe how a creative picture of systemic organization lets us map culture's dynamic, living evolutionary story.

Chapter Four turns to questions of human relationship and human identity. It confronts how the ways we have before thought about human connections of all sorts—whether relationships between nations, between leaders and followers, or between friends or lovers—have been "mythologized," based on projecting parts of our cognitive complexity onto others. And it examines how Cultural Maturity's more systemic holding of reality makes possible more complete kinds of relationships in all parts of our personal and collective lives. Chapter Four also confronts how past notions of identity have, in a similar way, been partial at best. It introduces what Creative Systems Theory calls the Myth of the Individual, and looks at how the theory's more systemic picture of what it means to be a person challenges many traditional assumptions of psychological thought.

Chapter Five focuses on the more general question of what makes something true. It highlights the essential recognition that intelligence has multiple aspects and describes the dramatic changes that follow from consciously drawing on the whole of that multiplicity. It also introduces the most basic of Creative Systems truth notions, what the theory calls Whole-Person/Whole-System patterning concepts. And it examines various ways that our thinking about what is true can go astray as we look to the future. Chapter Five concludes by describing specific approaches that can be used to address truth in the needed more complete sense.

Chapter Six turns to the critical sense in which culturally mature truth is contextual. When truths are based on ideology, we assume they are eternal and invariant. With culturally mature perspective, we better see how what makes something true depends on when and where we look. The chapter's reflections further expand on the kind of temporal, developmental relativity addressed in Chapter Three—what Creative Systems Theory calls Patterning in Time. And they go on to introduce concepts that address contextual relativity in the here and now—what the theory calls Patterning in Space. They also look at how, in a way unique to the theory, we can understand these two kinds of contextual differences as having related origins.

Chapter Seven delves into one of the most interesting and surprising outcomes with Cultural Maturity's cognitive changes, how they make it possible to address numerous questions that in times past have either left us baffled or produced limited, and ultimately unhelpful answers. This includes really quite ultimate questions. I will draw on Creative Systems Theory's particular vantage to briefly engage three such big-picture quandaries: the apparent contradiction between free will and determinism, the historically conflicting explanations of science and religion, and how we might best reconcile contrasting pictures of existence as a whole.

This book makes an important addition to the approaches I've used in other settings. Having the ideas of Creative Systems Theory documented in detail as I have in other books certainly has a purpose. And it is important too to appreciate that the theory's core insights, at least when we are ready for them, can feel like common sense. But it is just as important to recognize how new this needed new kind of common sense ultimately is, and with this, the foundational importance of that kind of newness. By the end of the book, it should be clear that the "growing up" as a species that Cultural Maturity's cognitive reordering produces is what our future depends on. It should also be clear that more detailed notions at least similar to those of Creative Systems Theory will be essential if we are to make good decisions going forward. I write the book as a further contribution toward making today's needed leap in understanding realizable—and the obvious task of our time.

CHAPTER ONE

Creative Systems Theory and the Concept of Cultural Maturity —A Brief Introduction

Given that readers may not be familiar with the contributions of Creative Systems Theory and the concept of Cultural Maturity, I will provide a brief introduction. Without a basic sense of the territory these notions cover and their conceptual foundations, it will be hard to fully appreciate what in them is new. And we will need to spend a bit of time with each. To understand one deeply, you must also understand the others.

I first formally introduced Creative Systems Theory and the concept of Cultural Maturity nearly forty years ago with my book *The Creative Imperative*.[1] We can put their achievements succinctly. The more specific concept of Cultural Maturity, in addressing the particular changes that define the evolutionary tasks of our time, offers a new kind of guiding narrative able to replace Modern Age beliefs. It also describes new kinds of skills and capacities that will be needed if we are to effectively make our way, and it clarifies the importance of thinking with a newly possible kind of systemic completeness. Creative Systems Theory provides a multifaceted set of tools for making our way in this new territory of experience. The theory has its foundation in the recognition that what most makes us who we are is the richness and complexity of our meaning-making, toolmaking—we could say simply "creative"— natures. The theory expands on this basic recognition to produce an overarching framework for understanding that reflects Cultural Maturity's more complete kind of perspective.

---

1 Charles M. Johnston, MD, *The Creative Imperative: Human Growth and Planetary Evolution*, Celestial Arts, 1984.

Cultural Maturity and the Changes That Make It Possible

I find it helpful to think of the changes that produce culturally mature understanding in a couple of steps. In the end, they reflect aspects of a single mechanism, but looking at them separately assists us in getting started.

The first change process gives the concept its name. Cultural Maturity produces a new, more mature relationship between culture and the individual. Always in times past, culture has functioned like a parent in the lives of individuals, offering us clear rules to live by. Such cultural absolutes have provided a sense of shared identity and connectedness with others. They have also protected us from life's very real uncertainties and immense complexities. But cultural absolutes are today serving us less and less well. They are also having diminishing influence.

This loss of past collective rules has two-sided implications. It reveals possibilities that before now we could not have considered. But at the same time, it can bring a disturbing sense of absence. Clearly something more is needed. If what we witness today reflects only a loss of past parental guideposts, we have problems. New possibility would be only of the postmodern—anything-goes, everybody-gets-their-own-truth—sort. What might seem to be freedom would produce instead only a loss of order and a dangerous kind of aimlessness.

The second kind of change process is what makes today's loss of past absolutes anything to celebrate. Cultural Maturity is not just about leaving behind familiar assumptions. It involves developmentally predicted cognitive changes. It turns out that the same change mechanisms that generate today's loss of past truths also create the potential for new, more mature ways of understanding. One way to think of culturally mature thought is that it is post-postmodern.

Creative Systems Theory uses an ungainly (but quite precise) term—Integrative Meta-perspective—to describe the new vantage that comes with Cultural Maturity's cognitive reordering. Integrative Meta-perspective involves, first, a more complete kind of stepping back from our complex natures. This stepping back creates both greater awareness and the ability to distance ourselves from culture's past parental role. And, second, Integrative Meta-perspective produces a new and deeper kind of engagement with the whole of our cognitive complexity, all the diverse aspects of who we are. The result is not just further abstraction, but the more fully embodied kind of understanding that is needed for mature decision-making.

We will come back for a closer look shortly. For now, it is enough to appreciate that Cultural Maturity's cognitive reordering, by allowing us to both more fully step back from and more deeply engage the whole of how we understand, lets us think in ways that are more encompassing and complete than was possible in times past. We could say more systemic—or simply more wise. I often use the metaphor of a box of crayons. The crayons represent systemic aspects. The box represents the more encompassing vantage. Integrative Meta-perspective lets us step back and draw more consciously—and deeply—on the whole box.

New Questions and New Human Capacities

I've suggested that addressing critical questions before us will require new kinds of human capacities. One of the best arguments for the concept of Cultural Maturity is that Cultural Maturity's cognitive reordering makes needed new capacities possible. Noting a few of them helps affirm the importance of the concept of Culturally Maturity and highlights some of where its changes take us.

Accepting a newly ultimate kind of responsibility: As we leave behind thinking of culture as a symbolic parent, we necessarily assume a new depth of responsibility—not just for our actions, but for the truths we draw on.

Getting beyond the ideological, simple-answer beliefs of times past: Creative Systems Theory defines ideology as any belief that takes a single crayon in the systemic box (or several crayons in collusion[2]) and confuses it with the whole of truth. Culturally mature understanding leaves behind not just the shared truths of particular cultural periods, but also the opposed ideological beliefs we find at specific points in time. It helps us address questions of all sorts with a new kind of systemic sophistication.

Learning to engage relationships in more complete ways: Creative Systems Theory describes how relationships of all sorts—from those between nations, to those that define leadership, to those we find with friendship or love—have always before been based on projection. Some of these projections demonize, others idealize. The theory also

---

2 See Chapter Five.

describes how Integrative Meta-perspective's more systemic vantage helps us re-own the projections that before have produced such mythologized perceptions. The importance of this capacity is most obvious when we look at how it offers a way beyond the kind of "chosen-people/evil-other" beliefs that have been the basis for war. But it is just as pertinent to the most intimate of connectings. With Cultural Maturity's cognitive reordering, we become better able to act in the world as whole systems, and to engage other systems as whole systems.[3]

Learning to better tolerate complexity and uncertainty: Questions of every kind today are confronting us with new complexities and uncertainties. Because Integrative Meta-perspective more directly draws on our own systemic complexity, it helps us better make sense of and tolerate complexity in the world around us. And for a related reason, Cultural Maturity's changes make us more comfortable in uncertainty's presence. When we engage understanding more fully, uncertainty becomes intrinsic to any deep understanding of truth. Creative Systems Theory goes further to describe how both complexity and uncertainty are necessary ingredients in cognition's "creative" workings.

Better appreciating the fact of real limits: The Modern Age story was heroic (or more precisely, heroic/romantic). We celebrated a world without limits. Increasingly, we recognize that if we are not more attentive to real limits, we are doomed. Integrative Meta-perspective's more encompassing vantage clarifies how, whatever our concern might be, limits in the end come with the territory. The greater maturity in the face of real limits that comes with Integrative Meta-perspective applies to real limits of every sort—limits to what we can do (as with environmental limits), limits to what we can know and predict (as we so often find with risk assessment), and limits to what we can be for one another (as with culturally mature relationships of all sorts). It also reveals how a mature acknowledgement of limits, rather than limiting us, in the end increases possibility.

Learning to think about what matters in more systemically complete ways: With Integrative Meta-perspective, we become newly able to address significance in ways that reflect the whole of who we are and the whole of whatever we might wish to consider. For example, moral decisions of all sorts

---

3 See Chapter Four.

become less about choosing between good and evil than about acknowledging competing goods and discerning where the most life-affirming choices ultimately lie. And as relationships of all sorts require us to step beyond two-halves-make-a-whole projective dynamics, in a similar way, Integrative Meta-perspective lets us more directly discern when a human connection enhances life. This new capacity applies most broadly to the critical task of rethinking advancement. Our times demand that we think about wealth and progress in ways that are more encompassing and complete.[4]

Better understanding how events happen in a context—particularly in the context of our time in culture's story: Thinking that can serve us going forward must help us make more dynamic and nuanced kinds of distinctions. Of particular importance, it must help us be more attentive to context. With culturally mature truth, the "when" and the "where" are always as important as the "what." Such contextual relativity is wholly different from relativity of the postmodern, anything-goes sort. Culturally mature understanding allows us to make highly precise discernments that are precise exactly because they take contextual nuances into account. We can think of Creative Systems Theory's framework for understanding purpose, change, and interrelationship in human systems as a set of tools for making such context-specific discernments.[5]

Integrative Meta-perspective

A closer look at the cognitive reorganization that underlies Cultural Maturity's changes helps us appreciate why such new capacities are a result. It also ties these capacities more directly to Creative Systems Theory's developmental framework. I've described how Integrative Meta-perspective involves at once more fully stepping back from and more deeply engaging the whole of our human complexity. Reflecting briefly on a couple of ways of thinking about that complexity—the role of polarity in how we think and the fact of intelligence's multiplicity—provides important beginning insight.

First, let's consider polarity. In Chapter Three, we will look at how each chapter in culture's story to this point has framed truth in terms

---

4 See Chapter Two.

5 See Chapter Six.

of qualities set in polar juxtaposition (for example, in modern times, mind versus body, leader versus follower, or science versus religion). Robert Frost observed that "It almost scares a man the way things come in pairs." With Cultural Maturity's cognitive reordering, we both step back from and more deeply engage past either/or relationships. In the process, we become able to appreciate them as aspects of larger systemic realities.

Creative Systems Theory brings detail to what we see. As a start, it addresses why we see polarity in the first place. After proposing that what most makes us human is our meaning-making, toolmaking, creative prowess, it goes on to describe how our cognitive mechanisms are designed to support this capacity for innovation. Specifically with regard to polarity, it describes how the fact that we think in polar terms follows directly from this creative picture. In Chapter Three we will examine how we find the same progression of polar relationships with creative/formative change of all sorts—from an act of invention, to personal psychological development, to the evolution of culture. Put most briefly, this progression begins with a newly created aspect budding off from its original context. Then, with each succeeding stage in formative process's first half, polar aspects become more separate, juxtaposing in evolving, creatively predicted ways. With the second, more mature half of any formative process, polarities reconcile to create a new and larger whole. We come to experience the newly created entity now as "second nature." When applied at a cultural scale, this second-half result has critical implications for understanding our time. The way Integrative Meta-perspective helps us get our minds around apparent polar opposites—here at the largest of scales—is a predicted consequence of our time in culture's evolving creative story.

We don't need Creative Systems Theory's detailed formulations to appreciate the basic relationship between polarity and Integrative Meta-perspective. F. Scott Fitzgerald proposed that the sign of a first-rate intelligence (we might say a mature intelligence) is the ability to hold two contradictory truths simultaneously in mind without going mad. His reference was to personal maturity, but this capacity is such an inescapable part of culturally mature perspective that we could almost say it defines it.

One of the simplest ways to think about how culturally mature perspective changes the way we understand draws on the basic observation that needed new understandings of every sort "bridge" polar assumptions from times past. I organized my early book *Necessary Wisdom* around this basic observation.[6] We can think of Cultural Maturity's point of departure as itself a "bridging" dynamic. We step back and see the relationship of culture and the individual in more encompassing terms. Cultural Maturity "bridges" ourselves and our societal contexts (or, put another way, ourselves and final truth). It is through this most fundamental "bridging" that we leave behind society's past parental function.

This most encompassing linkage holds within it a multitude of more local "bridgings." Nothing more characterized the last century's defining conceptual advances than how they linked previously unquestioned polar truths. Physics' new picture provocatively circumscribed the realities of matter and energy, space and time, and object with its observer. New understandings in biology better linked humankind with the natural world, and by reopening timeless questions about life's origins, joined the purely physical with the organic. And the ideas of modern psychology, neurology, and sociology have provided an increasingly integrated picture of the workings of conscious with unconscious, mind with body, self with society, and more.

If the relationship between "bridging" and Cultural Maturity is to make ultimately useful sense, it is important to include a couple of critical distinctions. We need, first, to clearly distinguish between personal maturity and Cultural Maturity. The ability to hold contradictory truths that F. Scott Fitzgerald observed is a characteristic of wise thought at any time in history. In contrast, none of the defining "bridgings" from the last century that I just noted would have made sense before now. The "bridging" of cultural realities that the concept of Cultural Maturity describes is specifically a phenomenon of our time.

We must also avoid confusing "bridging" as I am using the term with more familiar outcomes (which is why I put the word in quotes). The result is wholly different from averaging or compromise, walking some white line in the middle of a road. And of particular importance if we are not to confuse Cultural Maturity with ideas that it is not at all about, the result is fundamentally different from simple oneness, the

---

6 Charles M. Johnston, MD, *Necessary Wisdom: Meeting the Challenge of a New Cultural Maturity*, Celestial Arts, 1991.

collapsing of one pole into the other that we commonly see with more spiritual interpretations. "Bridging" in this sense is about consciously drawing on the whole creative box of crayons.

Framing Cultural Maturity's cognitive reordering in terms of intelligence's multiplicity provides further nuance and also helps us better put the changes that result—and their significance—in historical perspective. Creative Systems Theory highlights how intelligence has multiple parts. Besides our rationality (in which we take appropriate pride), intelligence has other aspects, some more emotional or symbolic, others more sensory. Most of what Creative Systems Theory has to say about our diverse ways of knowing must wait for later chapters,[7] but certain observations are specifically relevant.

Especially pertinent is Creative Systems Theory's explanation for why we have multiple intelligences. We come back to the theory's claim that what makes us particular as creatures is our creative proclivities. Creative Systems Theory delineates how our various intelligences work together to support and drive our dramatic toolmaking, meaning-making capacities. As we see with the evolution of polar dynamics, we find a parallel intelligence-specific progression with every kind of human formative process—be it invention, individual development, the growth of a relationship, or, of particular importance for these reflections, the evolution of culture. Different aspects of intelligence and different relationships between intelligences most define experience at different creative stages. This observation provides the basis for Creative Systems Theory's framework for understanding change in human systems.

This recognition also has consequences of a philosophical and paradigmatic sort. I've proposed that Creative Systems Theory is significant not just because it provides new conceptual tools for making our way, but also because it successfully takes us beyond the kind of thinking that has defined Modern Age understanding. Enlightenment thinkers such as Newton and Descartes described reality as a great clockworks. Machine-model thinking has given us not just industrial advancement and great scientific advancement, but also modern institutional forms and our modern concept of the individual. But it presents real problems if we wish to talk about ourselves as systems. The creative frame that

---

7 In particular, see Chapter Five.

serves as the theory's foundation helps us put the mechanistic assumptions of times past (along with their more romantic complements[8]) in historical perspective. And it specifically takes us beyond them. By drawing on this dynamic and generative approach to understanding, the theory is able to provide highly delineated formulations that directly reflect the fact that we are living—and human—beings.

A more historical look at Integrative Meta-perspective using the lens of intelligence's multiplicity helps fill out the conceptual leap that produces culturally mature understanding. Modern Age thought similarly had its origins in a new kind of cognitive orientation. And stepping back from previous ways of knowing was a big part of it. We became better able to step back from the more mystical sensibilities that gave us the beliefs of the Middle Ages. Along with this more general stepping back, rationality came to have a newly central significance. The rational now stood clearly separate from the subjective aspects of experience and became specifically allied with conscious awareness. The result was a new, as-if-from-a-balcony sense of clarity and objectivity. This, combined with the new belief in the individual as logical choice-maker that accompanied it, produced all the great advances of the Modern Age.

While Modern Age thought was a grand achievement, Integrative Meta-perspective's stepping back represents a wholly different sort of accomplishment. Awareness comes to stand more fully separate from the whole of our intelligence's systemic complexity—including the rational. Integrative Meta-perspective offers that we might step back equally from aspects of ourselves that before we might have treated as objective and those that we before thought of as subjective. In the process, it offers that we might better step back from the whole of intelligence.

And there is more. Culturally mature understanding requires not just that we be aware that intelligence has multiple aspects, but that in a whole new sense we embody each of these aspects. It directly draws on all of our diverse ways of knowing. Culturally mature understanding requires

---

8 What we see with the eighteenth-century philosophical thinking of Jean-Jacques Rousseau, in later artistic and literary contributions, and often today with more left-leaning political ideologies and New Age conclusions.

thinking in a rational sense—indeed, it expands rationality's role. But just as much it involves more directly plumbing the more feeling, imagining, and sensing aspects of who we are. And this is the case as much for the most rigorous of hard theory as when our concerns are more personal. Making sense of most anything about us—the values we hold, the nature of identity, what it means to have human relationship—increasingly requires this more encompassing kind of understanding.

An important result with Cultural Maturity might at first seem contradictory. On one hand, because culturally mature perspective draws on multiple, often conflicting aspects of who we are, its conclusions are less absolute and once-and-for-all than those we are used to. But at the same time, we can appropriately argue that culturally mature understanding is more "objective" than what it replaces. Certainly it is more complete. Enlightenment thought might have claimed ultimate objectivity, but this was in fact objectivity of only a limited sort. Besides leaving culture's parental status untouched, it left experience as a whole divided— objective (in the old sense) set opposed to subjective, mind set opposed to body, thoughts set opposed to feelings. We cannot ultimately claim to be objective if we have left out half of the evidence. Culturally mature objectivity is of a more specifically all-the-crayons-in-the-box sort.

Equally important is a further result that I've hinted at that might also seem contradictory. While culturally mature thought requires that we take into account greater complexity and uncertainty, when we are ready for it, there are also ways in which it is more straightforward—and arguably simpler—than what it replaces. Ideological beliefs of times past have protected us from life's easily overwhelming complexities, but they have achieved this by distorting perception. Cultural Maturity's vantage helps us come closer to seeing things for just how they are. It is this that has me refer to culturally mature understanding as a "new common sense."

The Dilemma of Trajectory and Transitional Absurdity

The fact that we can understand Cultural Maturity in terms of developmentally predicted cognitive changes points toward an important additional implication. If Cultural Maturity's cognitive changes are as potential built into who we are, the likelihood that we can thrive and prosper in times ahead increases significantly. And if this is a cognitive reordering that we can actively practice and facilitate, that likelihood increases further. This picture supports being legitimately optimistic about what may lie ahead.

But there are also plenty of reasons to have doubts about the future. Possibility is not destiny. A couple of additional Creative Systems concepts help frame the larger challenge. They are important to touch on at least briefly if the precarious circumstances we so often confront in our times are to make sense—and certainly if humanity's more long-term challenge is to make sense. We will come back later for a closer look at each of them.[9]

The first Creative Systems Theory calls the Dilemma of Trajectory. The Dilemma of Trajectory clarifies how our times demand something more than just letting go of one cultural stage and moving to another. It describes how the challenges that confront us today bring into question the whole developmental orientation that has before defined growth and truth. The Dilemma of Trajectory makes something at least similar to what the concept of Cultural Maturity suggests inescapably necessary.

We can frame the circumstance it presents most simply using the language of polarity. Each stage in culture to this point has been defined by greater distinction between polar opposites and a greater emphasis on difference more generally. (In tribal times, connectedness to nature and tribe was primary; today it is materiality and individuality that prevails.) We can also frame the Dilemma of Trajectory in terms of intelligence's multiplicity. We've evolved from times in which the more creatively germinal aspects of intelligence—the body and the imagination—most informed experience (to be part of a tribe is to know the tribal dances and rituals) to times in which the rational—with a limited contribution from the emotional—holds the much larger influence (enter the Age of Reason). Alternatively, we can describe this evolution using a more general language drawn from the study of myth. Culture's story has taken us from times in which archetypally feminine influences ruled to times in which the archetypally masculine is much more the defining presence.[10]

---

9 See Chapters Two and Three.

10 This conceptual language comes from the thinking of psychiatrist Carl Jung. Because of the insights it provides, CST often makes use of it. I will always include the modifier "archetypally" even though doing so might

With our time, this organizing trajectory has reached an extreme. Truth has come to be defined almost exclusively by difference (for example, we view objective and subjective as wholly separate worlds), we equate rationality with understanding, and extreme archetypally masculine values prevail (such as those of the marketplace and the technological). The Dilemma of Trajectory alerts us to how going further in this direction would not benefit us. Indeed, there is an important sense in which going forward as we have has really stopped being an option. We would not do well if we lost what remaining connection we have with nature, our bodies, or the more receptive aspects of experience that form the basis of human relationship. Proceeding further in this direction would irretrievably alienate us from aspects of who we are that are essential to being human.

So what are we to do? We could go back—a proposal that is at least implied in certain kinds of social advocacy and more popular thinking about the future. But as I will strongly emphasize, going back is not any more likely to get us where we need to go. Unless there is a further option, the human experiment could be at a conclusion. By reconciling the Dilemma of Trajectory, Integrative Meta-perspective offers a possible way forward. And it is a way forward that points toward an essential kind of human realization and fulfillment.

The second additional concept relates to an observation that could seem to prove the concept of Cultural Maturity wrong. A lot that we

---

seem cumbersome, as it is important to clearly distinguish qualities we all share from conclusions we might have about men or women. (Men and women each embody both kinds of characteristics.) In Chapter Four I will come back to the importance of this distinction when addressing questions that relate specifically to either gender or identity.

I've mentioned that with rare exception the development of CST predated my encounters with other thinkers who have asked related questions. Carl Jung is one of those exceptions. Creative Systems Theory's initial insights preceded contact with his thinking (and CST in its current form goes well beyond his conclusions), but in reading his works during medical school, I saw that there were important relationships between his project and what I was trying to do with the theory. In particular, I saw the importance of his recognition that unconscious aspects of our psychology are not just repositories for repressed content, but ultimately generative. His ideas helped motivate me to train as a psychiatrist.

see in today's world might appear to be almost the opposite of what the concept predicts—for example, increasing political and social polarization, widespread denial with regard to essential limits-related challenges such as climate change and the extinction of species, and today's growing rates of suicide, addiction, and gun violence. Given that we find so much in contemporary human behavior that can seem ludicrous, it can be hard to believe that getting wiser as a species is a possibility.

It may not be. But as I will come back to, it turns out that much that we see today is consistent with what we would expect to find as we begin to engage Cultural Maturity's demands. Creative Systems Theory describes how our times should be characterized not just by new possibility, but also by distorted ways of thinking and acting. It calls this particular kind of ludicrousness Transitional Absurdity. Some Transitional Absurdities simply reflect where the Dilemma of Trajectory naturally takes us. Others come from "overshooting the mark"—extending assumptions that have long since stopped being pertinent. And others still reflect regression in the face of our time's easily overwhelming demands. In each case, unhelpful—even quite crazy—responses are the result. Like it or not, we live in awkward, in-between times. The important recognition is that, whatever the origins of today's absurdities, with sufficient courage and persistence, Cultural Maturity works as an antidote.

The Importance of Evidence

A radical concept like Cultural Maturity requires good evidence, as does the conclusion that more encompassing ideas like those of Creative Systems Theory might be possible. I will give primary attention in the chapters ahead to what makes these notions new, but the explanations in each case will also provide evidence that the concept of Cultural Maturity and the ideas of Creative Systems Theory are accurate and important.

Observations made to this point provide a start. The fact that Cultural Maturity's changes make needed new capacities possible supports the conclusion that something like what the concept describes will at least be necessary. Creative Systems Theory's developmental framework—whether we approach it through the lens of polarity or through the evolution of intelligence—provides a more conceptual kind of evidence. And more specific Creative Systems Theory notions like the Dilemma of Trajectory and Transitional Absurdity make the need for something at least similar to what the concept of Cultural Maturity describes impossible to escape.

For me, the most compelling evidence for Cultural Maturity's thesis—and with it, for the importance of the kind of overarching thought that Creative Systems Theory provides—is the simplest. I don't see other ways of framing the human tasks ahead that are similarly consistent with a future that is healthy and vital. The needed stretch is considerable and there is no guarantee that we will succeed in making it. But we don't really have the option of failing. If I have not missed something important, working to realize Cultural Maturity's changes and the more complete kind of thinking and acting that they make possible becomes the only option going forward, the only game in town.

CHAPTER TWO

Not Just a New Chapter in the Human Story, but a New Kind of Story

Reflecting more deeply on the concept of Cultural Maturity helps provide a solid foundation for addressing how these notions are not just new, but new in a radical and significant way. Cultural Maturity is a kind of idea that before now would not have made sense to us. And if before now we did begin to make sense of it, we likely could not have tolerated its implications.

Previous reflections have made a solid beginning. I've described how culturally mature perspective takes us beyond making culture a mythic parent. I've also observed how Cultural Maturity's changes replace the cognitive structures that have produced the contrasting objectivist and romantic beliefs of Modern Age thought with a more complete and integrative kind of cognitive organization. I've pointed toward how such Integrative Meta-perspective offers that we might think in ways that better reflect our living human natures. And I've noted how the leap that culturally mature understanding represents makes possible the capacities needed if we are to effectively address the essential challenges before us as a species.

Succeeding with this leap is no small accomplishment. For me, the demanding nature of the challenge becomes immediately apparent when attempting to teach about Cultural Maturity and its implications. I can describe in detail the cognitive reordering that makes culturally mature understanding possible. And I can give people the opportunity to try out needed new capacities. But unless people are ready, none of this will get them there. Such difficulties might seem to contradict my assertion that where culturally mature understanding takes us is straightforward. We find needed clarification in the recognition that while Cultural Maturity's new developmental steps require more than most people can presently easily handle, when they are timely, they can seem quite obvious. Indeed, they can take place quite well on their own without any instruction. I find delight in watching how the way a person holds experience changes—quickly and dramatically—when the needed new kind of cognitive organization begins to click into place.

Here I'll come at the concept of Cultural Maturity's newness in a handful of ways that help further fill out what makes it radical. First, I'll briefly contrast it with other ways of thinking about the future and the tasks of our time. Next, I will address what makes its unique perspective important in terms of its practical consequences. I will then turn to the evolution of narrative, expanding on Cultural Maturity's particular place in history's ever-changing story of who we are and how reality works. I will reflect some on how the analogy implied in the phrase "Cultural Maturity" helps us appreciate the Dilemma of Trajectory. And finally, I will focus specifically on how Cultural Maturity redefines human advancement, not just for now but in an important sense for our future more generally.

What Cultural Maturity Is Not

Let's take a moment for some basic compare-and-contrast observations. The simple claim that the concept of Cultural Maturity helps us make sense of what our times ask of us is at least of significance. Here I've gone further to assert that if something like what the concept of Cultural Maturity describes is not basically correct, it is hard to be legitimately hopeful about our human future. This assertion begs an essential question: Just how is Cultural Maturity different from more familiar notions about what may lie ahead for the species? If more common ways of framing contemporary and future challenges ultimately fail, then the concept of Cultural Maturity becomes new and significant in a particularly consequential sense.

Certainly what the concept of Cultural Maturity suggests is different from what we find with "we've arrived" views that assume that if Modern Age beliefs are not sufficient, only a little refinement will be required. It emphasizes the need for a further chapter in the human story—both further, more mature ways of understanding and more developed kinds of institutional structures. The concept of Cultural Maturity is also fundamentally different from most views that see the future in terms of change. The most familiar of such views make the future's task continuing to progress as we have—with the focus most often on technological advancement. This is how the average person tends to think about what lies ahead, as do most self-described futurists. With the best of such thinking there is the essential recognition that risks as well as benefits accompany any new advancement, but the general picture is onward and upward.

Views that are more specific about what changes might involve, particularly those that take us in anything like a new direction, tend to divide into those where conclusions are more utopian and those that are more dystopian. Sometimes we find extreme versions, but most such views are more tempered, with utopian or dystopian sentiments only implied in their assumptions. Any ideological belief—any way of thinking that gives particular crayons in the box a monopoly on truth—will be of this sort. It will assume that if we heed our beliefs, all will be well.

Comparing the concept of Cultural Maturity with utopian and dystopian views provides a good way to clarify what makes its insights particular—and radical. The more extreme of utopian views provide the clearest contrast. They themselves tend to be of two kinds, those of a more techno-utopian and those of a more spiritually utopian sort. Each in its own way leaves us fundamentally short of what the future asks of us.

Techno-utopian notions represent an ultimate extension of the Modern Age onward-and-upward story. They assume that future invention will save us. In doing so, they leave us in denial about the nature of much that is most important in the challenges that we face. Future invention will be critical. But techno-utopian simplemindedness could well be the end of us. Spiritual utopian views promise some ultimate salvation. That may be for a chosen few, as with certain fundamentalist beliefs. Or, as with more New Age notions, they may propose that reaching some "higher consciousness" or some modern-day version of enlightenment will lift us above the troubles of our times. Such views are less likely to put us directly at risk. But the naivety of the answers they suggest in the end only distracts us from the significance of today's challenges. Later I will describe how spiritually framed solutions commonly have their roots in ways of thinking seen frequently throughout history, most often with early stages in culture. In contrast, understanding that follows from Integrative Meta-perspective and its new kind of cognitive organization is of a wholly new sort.

Dystopian conclusions suggest an opposite fate to these more cheery scenarios. We find them with both religious notions of an impending apocalypse and more cynical social, political, and intellectual positions that see the species somehow going to hell in a handbasket. What the concept of Cultural Maturity describes is again fundamentally different. It points toward how calamitous results are certainly possible—and essentially inescapable if we don't engage needed next steps. But it also suggests options that are not just positive, but radically significant.

We can miss the fact that more everyday ideological conclusions are utopian. But in identifying with particular crayons in the systemic box, they share the assumption that a particular kind of belief provides the needed final answer. Because they most often identify with one half of a polarity, we can think of them as at once utopian and dystopian: utopian in making their own position final truth and dystopian in assuming that an opposite position will lead us dangerously astray. In the end, they are just as absolutist as more extreme versions and just as much leave us short.

We could put together a long list of utopian and dystopian views of a more tempered sort. My list would include everyday ideological advocacies such as the positions of the political right or the political left. (As the beliefs of the Right and the Left today more and more often each retreat to their populist extremes, the underlying absolutism becomes increasingly obvious and shrill.) I would also include views that identify with either science or religion not as aspects of truth, but as final truths—the contrasting views of scientism and fundamentalism. I would include too the often ardently held ideological beliefs common in particular fields. On learning about thinking in domains far distant from my own, I've often been struck by how often conclusions in diverse spheres manifest as related juxtapositions of mutually exclusive, single-crayon-in-the-box beliefs. We can also look to more general beliefs about belief. In Chapter Six I will describe how we can think of the whole of philosophy as an evolving series of arguments for more right-hand and more left-hand metaphysical answers. Philosophically framed views of the future tend to follow in these traditions.

Cultural Maturity represents a wholly different kind of concept than what we find with any of these ways of thinking about the future. Certainly, it confronts beliefs that make current assumptions sufficient. And, just as much, it ultimately challenges utopian and dystopian beliefs even of the more tempered sort. In fact it challenges the idea that any of them represent anything really new. Utopian and dystopian notions all come from long lineages of belief. They reflect extensions from what we have known, with utopian conclusions celebrating some final realization and dystopian views lamenting failure at these same historically familiar goals. In contrast, what Cultural Maturity's needed "growing up" in how we think and act describes is fundamentally new. I've described how culturally mature perspective provides the ability to hold reality in more encompassing ways than before has been an option. Cultural Maturity is about consciously drawing on the whole box of crayons and applying the larger understanding that results to our personal and collective life choices. This is not something we have seen before.

Most immediately this result takes us beyond other ways of framing the tasks ahead in being more complete. It is also different in providing effective guidance for addressing challenges before us. And, importantly, it is different in a further way that might seem a paradox but that is central to understanding what makes Cultural Maturity radical in its newness. While culturally mature perspective takes us radically forward, it is also in an important sense more "ordinary" than what we have known.

The precise developmental analogy provides clarification. Later in this chapter we will return for a closer look. For now it is enough to emphasize that Cultural Maturity finds its personal development parallel not in becoming an adult, but in the demands of the more mature kind of maturity needed as we confront the second half of our individual lives.[1] Developmental challenges in the first half of life paint a picture of onward-and-upward achievement—the task is to give our budding personal existence form and delineation. Second-half-of-life developmental challenges are different. When we succeed with them we find greater self-awareness, increased perspective, and a new sense

---

1 Because of this essential difference, I will always put the phrase "growing up" in quotes.

of proportion—and even wisdom—in our lives. These are profound accomplishments, but they are accomplishments of a more humble sort. They reflect a kind of realization, but they are not about final truths, of either the more or less hopeful sort. They are simply about better seeing what is, more clearly. Musician Miles Davis once observed that "You have to play for a long time to play like yourself." His words beautifully captured such second-half "ordinariness."

Cultural Maturity's changes are similarly about something at once more profound and more humble than what we have known. As such, they are ultimately more radical. Utopian and dystopian beliefs can seem radical. Certainly they make for ready slogans. But Cultural Maturity's more humble kind of result represents a more fundamental challenge to familiar assumptions. We can think of it as radical twice over. In being something new to our time, Integrative Meta-perspective's more whole-box-of-crayons picture is at least as radical as what we have seen with previous major cultural change points. And in the sense that we can think of its more integrative picture as more ordinary—simply about better holding the whole of who we are and how we understand—it is radical in a way that we have not witnessed before.

Why It Matters

The claim that Cultural Maturity's new picture of possibility takes us forward in a way that succeeds in addressing the tasks of our time is critical. Were this not the case, there would be no reason to consider it. And the observation that other ways of thinking about the future fail in this regard brings the significance of the concept into focus in a particularly tangible and direct way. It turns out that the wholly new kind of understanding that the concept of Cultural Maturity represents will be needed to effectively engage any of the most important challenges ahead for us as a species. That includes addressing concrete risks that could well be our undoing; taking important steps forward in how we understand and act; and, related to both, the challenge of crafting a story for our time sufficiently compelling to provide legitimate hope.

As the more concrete kind of challenge is easiest to articulate, I will begin there. Today we confront risks of multiple sorts that we appropriately think of as existential. They could be the end of us—and often sooner rather than later. The top four on my list: future use of weapons of mass destruction, climate change and its potential consequences, global pandemic, and digital technologies run amok. Earlier I listed some of the new human capacities that come with culturally mature understanding. It turns out that not only can culturally mature capacities help us address these challenges, existential consequences become essentially inevitable if we do not have such capacities available to us.

Weapons of mass destruction are becoming increasing available not just to advanced nations, but also to rogue states and terrorist groups. I suspect that nuclear weapons will again be used in the future, if not of a megaton scale, at least of a more limited sort or nuclear dirty bombs. And the future tragic use of weaponry of the biological or chemical sort is even more likely. These circumstances could well be the cause of our demise unless we can get beyond our past need to define identity in terms of chosen people and evil others. Quite exceptional culturally mature leadership will be needed if they are not to escalate into an ultimate kind of catastrophe.

With regard to climate change, we are already at a point where major consequences have become unavoidable. Today we are seeing increasingly frequent severe weather events, famines and water shortages, and a growing risk of wildfires around the world. And consequences of a specifically environmental sort will likely be the least of it. Migrations of distressed populations and the exacerbation of global poverty will greatly increase the likelihood of conflict. Restricting climate change to levels that we can adapt to will require the kind of conscious acknowledgement of real limits that Cultural Maturity makes possible. And effectively dealing with the consequences of climate change will demand other new Cultural Maturity–related capacities such as the ability to better assess risk and appreciating the essential role of context in making decisions.

The coronavirus pandemic has made the dangers of worldwide disease newly obvious. In times past, even though epidemics have played a major role in shaping history, when experts cautioned about this sort of risk, people have tended not to take warnings seriously. Again, an appreciation for limits, and not just to what we can do, but also to what we can know, will be essential if we are to effectively address this inescapable threat. So will be a greater capacity for foresight and greater wisdom in our assessment of risks if we are not to pay a high price for our shortsightedness.

The possible runaway consequences of new digital technologies may ultimately present the greatest existential risk. We are beginning to recognize such dangers today with how social media in combination with machine learning algorithms distort reality and generate discord. In Chapter Five, I will describe how the reason that machine learning presents danger is not the one most often cited, that in time it will become more intelligent than we are and come to rule us. In fact, in many ways it is already more intelligent than we are. The greater danger lies in how machine learning really has very little to do with human intelligence. I will propose that the only real antidote lies in us learning to manifest the unique kind of intelligence that makes us human in more conscious and mature ways.

While such concrete threats provide the most dramatic way to talk about Cultural Maturity's necessity, arguably we find greater ultimate significance in how Cultural Maturity's changes present new possibilities. This includes how Cultural Maturity's cognitive reordering brings a new sophistication to understanding in all parts of our lives. It also includes more specific—and often strikingly significant—kinds of advancement. Later I will describe how Cultural Maturity invites us to think about and engage relationships of all sorts in ways that both increase options and offer new kinds of fulfillment. We will look too at how Cultural Maturity's cognitive reordering expands our understanding of what it means to be an individual, and ultimately to what it means to be a person. It is not just that other ways of thinking about the future fail to successfully protect us from calamity; in the end, they keep us from recognizing the kinds of changes that may result in the greatest rewards going forward.

The third kind of challenge can be thought of as bringing the other two together. It has to do with where we are to find meaning in our time. For me as a psychiatrist, it provides particularly concrete support for the concept of Cultural Maturity. Past ways of thinking and acting have stopped providing a reliable sense of substance and fulfillment in people's lives. I introduced my short book *Hope and the Future* by describing a young man I had seen in therapy who had attempted to hang himself. It became strikingly clear as our work progressed that the hopelessness he felt was only in limited ways personal. It was more about the state of the world. He described having a hard time thinking of a future that he would want to be a part of.

I gave that book the subtitle, *"Confronting Today's Crisis of Purpose."* I've made the notion of a modern Crisis of Purpose a formal concept within Creative Systems Theory. I think of this crisis as a primary contributor to much that we find most disturbing in contemporary society—such rising rates of suicide, depression, addiction, obesity, and gun violence. For me, the most compelling argument for the concept of Cultural Maturity is that it offers a new North Star for our actions that is consistent not just with effective decision-making, but also with a meaningful existence.

Cultural Maturity and the Evolution of Narrative

The question of narrative—and its relationship to our experience of meaning—offers one of the best ways to make sense of the leap that Cultural Maturity's changes represent. We can turn to the stories we have told throughout history about ourselves, how the world works, and just what creates significance. I could as well have given *Hope and the Future* the subtitle "Confronting Today's Crisis of Narrative."

The big-picture perspective needed for a comparative look at narrative requires more of a stepping back than we are used to. But in important further ways, it helps fill out just what is new—and radical—in where the concept of Cultural Maturity takes us. Going way back, we find the stories of our animistic beginnings, tales based in our inseparable relationship with nature. With the rise of the early civilizations, our stories came to intertwine with the lives of great pantheons of gods.[2] Later in the West, we find the more theological and moral defining narratives of the Middle Ages.[3] I've framed the beginning emergence of Modern Age understanding in terms of newly objectivist/rationalist/materialist/individualist beliefs and their polar counterparts, but we could just as well think of modern understanding in terms of narrative.

---

2 In the East, understanding at this stage has often been framed more philosophically, as with Taoist and early Buddhist teachings. We saw something similar in the West with the more specifically philosophical teachings of the later stages of classical Greek thought.

3 We see a related new emphasis on moral and social considerations with Confucian thought in the East.

Modern Age narratives have juxtaposed two kinds of stories: heroic and romantic. Heroic narratives describe the overcoming of obstacles to realize some ultimate achievement. Romantic narratives describe some meeting—either personal or more encompassing—that results in emotional or spiritual oneness. Heroic and romantic narratives can work alone or together. Heroic and romantic narratives were not new to Modern Age thought, but they then came to manifest in a new, specifically individualistic form.[4] The most familiar of modern day societal beliefs—the American Dream, opposing political worldviews, the traditional assumptions of our various religions, conventional beliefs about relationships of all sorts, progress' promise of ever onward-and-upward scientific discovery and technological advancement—all reflect this specifically individualist kind of heroic/romantic narrative. But none are sufficient for the kinds of questions that we more and more confront today. At the least, each celebrates limitlessness when the acknowledgement of real limits has become key to moving forward.

Of particular importance for these reflections, in recent decades, we've also witnessed narratives of a more Transitional sort, ones that straddle the threshold into Cultural Maturity's new territory of experience. Earlier I used the word "postmodern" to describe this kind of story. Postmodern thought has its historical roots in European existentialism and has manifested more recently with social constructivist ideas in academia. Postmodern thought and culturally mature thought share certain similarities. The postmodernist appreciates that the cultural absolutes of times past no longer provide the benefit they once did. And in a related way to what we see with culturally mature perspective, postmodern conclusions recognize a newly multifaceted and often uncertain reality in which meaning is increasingly ours to determine.

But as we might expect with such "straddling" belief, postmodern thought only gets us part of the way. And it fails with what is ultimately the most consequential part of the task. It recognizes the limitations of the past's absolutist ideological beliefs, but it is capable of only a beginning grasp of what—if anything—might lie beyond them. Except in the best of formulations, it easily reduces to an anything-

---

4 Homer's Odyssey was certainly a heroic tale, but it was as much about the actions of gods and mythic forces as it was about the person of Ulysses.

goes, different-strokes-for-different-folks reality in which one truth is as good as another. Arbitrariness gets confused with significance.

Postmodern thought's limitations manifest in a couple of critical ways when it comes to the tasks ahead. Because its contribution provides little in the way of real direction, it proves helpless to address today's loss of guiding narrative in any deep way. And because postmodern theorists have an aversion to overarching conception, it undermines efforts to bring any real detail and sophistication to understanding.[5] If we are not careful, postmodern thinking becomes, in effect, but another kind of ideology (and a kind of ideology that is particularly tedious and difficult to counter).

The greatest danger if we fail at the task of narrative is not that we will believe things that really don't hold up to scrutiny, though there is that. Rather, it comes back to the Crisis of Purpose that I made reference to in describing my client who attempted to hang himself. As truth becomes anything we might choose, we easily end up feeling rudderless in what can seem like an essentially arbitrary world. And while new versions of utopian and dystopian truths may titillate and at least temporarily satisfy, in time they too prove inadequate. It is a danger compounded dramatically by how the artificial stimulation in the name of meaning so common in contemporary culture leaves us ever more distant from real significance. Arguably the greatest danger in our time is triviality.

Culturally mature understanding takes us beyond Transitional beliefs of all sorts. I've described how we can think of it as "post-postmodern." It affirms the best of postmodern insight—the importance of getting past the absolutist beliefs of times past and engaging experience more directly. But it doesn't stop there. Its cognitive changes make it possible not just to leave behind past ideological certainties, but also to bring ourselves more consciously and fully to the whole of experience. In the process, it offers that we might more fully engage the complexities of the world around us and think in more sophisticated ways. And by giving us a new and deeper sense of meaning in our experience of being human, it provides an answer to today's crisis of narrative.

---

5 Jean-François Lyotard famously described this as an "incredulity toward meta-narratives." (Jean-François Lyotard, *The Postmodern Condition*, University of Minnesota Press, 1984.)

In our time we see a variety of beliefs that can claim to take us forward but that on close examination reduce to new versions of past ideological conclusions. In Chapter Five I will describe how modern cognitive science, while it takes on questions that science before would not have considered, in the process often leaves us even more entangled in materialism's trap. New more spiritually framed views in a similar way often ask important questions, but more often than not they link conceptually to modern forms of philosophical idealism,[6] or to even earlier spiritual and philosophical beliefs. Contemporary humanistic notions are often put forward as solutions, but along with the more adamant of environmentalist, feminist, and "woke" social advocacy, they are best thought of as modern descendants of timeworn romantic beliefs.

Throughout the last century we have witnessed beginning contributions to culturally mature thought, certainly in specific fields, with many of them of significant importance. But it has not been a simple, smooth journey. The postmodern project, while it has in a sense taken us forward, at the same time has often served to take attention away from these beginnings. And I've noted how we've often seen regression over the last thirty years. This is most explicit with growing enmity and polarization around social/political concerns, but we see it in some way

---

6 Philosophical idealism views change as having an idealized end point. Modern expressions of philosophical idealism have both more social/political and more spiritual forms. Georg Hegel's views were of the first sort, as were those of Karl Marx. We find an often-cited more spiritual form of philosophical idealism in the thinking of French Jesuit priest and paleontologist Pierre Teilhard de Chardin, who postulated that culture evolves toward an ultimate "omega point." The nineteenth century German idealist Friedrich Schelling reached related conclusions. Contemporary cultural views that could be described as evolutionary often reflect the perspective of philosophical idealism, particularly of the more spiritual sort. As such, while they often have useful insights to provide about the past, they tend to be much less helpful when it comes to understanding current circumstance or addressing the future. In Chapter Five, I will delineate how the kinds of cognitive structures that produce philosophical idealism remain fundamentally short of what we find with Integrative Meta-perspective. In Chapter Six I will touch on one giveaway for the ultimately ideological nature of such notions, how they tend to give certain personality styles a leg up when it comes to being more developed or evolved.

in most every sphere of inquiry and understanding.[7] We reside in an awkward in-between time in which, at the same time, we are witnessing some of the most inspired of thinking, and much that leaves us far distant from where we need to go.

"Growing Up" and the Dilemma of Trajectory

I've made reference to a critical quandary that relates directly to my assertion that the concept of Cultural Maturity provides an answer to today's Crisis of Narrative. It also sheds light on the awkward in-between nature of current circumstances. It might seem a showstopper. I'm referring to what Creative Systems Theory calls the Dilemma of Trajectory, how continuing to go forward as we have threatens to distance us irretrievably from aspects of ourselves essential to being human. It is a critical recognition.

I've observed how we can understand formative processes in human systems in terms of the evolution of polarity. Each stage in any formative process's first half is defined by greater distinction between poles and a greater emphasis on difference more generally. At formative process's midpoint this defining impetus reaches an extreme. Going further in this direction stops giving us anything of value. Indeed, there is an important sense in which it really stops being possible at all. We face the Dilemma of Trajectory.

Further contrasting the two ways we use the word "maturity" with individual development both highlights this circumstance and clarifies how further options—indeed, rich and important options—might lie beyond it. I've noted that the analogy that gives Cultural Maturity its name refers to second-half-of-life maturity, the more complete kind of growing up that in potential gives us larger perspective, and even

---

7 A colleague who is a Catholic nun recently shared her disappointment that the kind of ecumenical conferences common in the later decades of the last century (that brought together people from far-flung faiths) had become rare. I've witnessed something similar in my own field. I remember a national gathering organized by psychiatrist Milton Ericsson in 1988 that invited the best thinkers from each of the often warring schools of psychological thought to join in conversation. I've not experienced anything of similar depth since. Late in the last century, books and newsletters that attempted to articulate post-partisan political perspective were also common.

wisdom. Personal development's first half is marked by processes that produce ever-greater individuality, independence, and authority over the world around us. This general direction of change defines growth as children and in becoming adults. But later it stops working. If we continue on as we have, life becomes increasingly absurd, at best a thin caricature of youth. Successfully engaging second-half-of-life developmental challenges produces changes of a specifically integrative sort. This is not to say that individuality becomes less—in fact, it continues to grow, often manifesting in particularly delightful and idiosyncratic ways. But when we successfully take on second-half-of-life developmental tasks, the tendency toward difference becomes counterbalanced by equally important integrative mechanisms.

With culture's story to this point, we've seen changes analogous to those we encounter with personal development's first half. In a similar way, we've witnessed a growing impetus toward individuality, independence, and authority. The invention of fire freed human migration. The Magna Carta affirmed basic human privilege. And our Modern Age has continued such appropriately proud advancement. The truths of our Modern Age have their foundation in increasing delineation of the individual will and growing independence from the constraints of nature and the irrational. The Declaration of Independence proclaimed the right of the individual to the pursuit of happiness. And the Industrial Age brought dramatic new expressions of human dominion and control. In their timeliness, such achievements could not have been more significant.

Today, as we find with the end of first-half dynamics in individual development, this trajectory has stopped benefitting us. While much of what we have reaped, and will continue to reap, from our ability to stand separate in the sense of individuality and autonomy of choice has been dramatically important, the future cries out as much for a new appreciation of how we are related, a fresh understanding of caring, community, and the common good. In a similar way, while culture's evolution has also brought with it increasing human control—over nature, over our own bodies, over life's deep mysteries—today almost the opposite seems equally a part of what is needed, a new humility to what we cannot control, a new sensitivity to when we should be listening as opposed to directing (whether the voice needing attention is the natural world, our tissues, or the unfathomable).

We confront profound questions—indeed, questions with god-like implications—but the authority needed to address them is not some ascension to a chair of final dominion (ourselves somehow becoming gods). It is also different from some further iteration of the Enlightenment's grand goal of bringing all of understanding into the pure light of awareness and realizing final control over the untamed. Indeed, many of the problems we face in today's world derive from just such hubristic notions of what right action is about. We are left in a pickle that cannot be resolved within the assumptions of our first kind of maturity. Any familiar notion of going forward threatens to take us in very wrong directions.

The Dilemma of Trajectory is significant not just because ignoring it will result in misguided actions. If it is accurate to think of cultural evolution as creative, proceeding further in this direction of distinction and separation leaves us at a dead end. Distinction and separation can only go so far. Cultural Maturity—or at least something that can produce changes similar to the more integrative mechanisms the concept describes—becomes the only real option.

We again see how the concept of Cultural Maturity is at once radical in its implications and common sense. It is radical in that it has no meaning if we limit ourselves to the beliefs of times past, or more precisely, to how our cognitive mechanisms have worked in times past. It is common sense in being more complete, about better addressing the whole of what we need to consider. It is also common sense because it reflects a kind of perspective and larger understanding that is developmentally right and timely—and inescapably necessary.

Redefining Human Advancement

Traditionally, we have defined advancement in terms of invention and material growth. The way Integrative Meta-perspective fundamentally challenges familiar notions of progress provides one of the best ways to grasp what is radically new with culturally mature understanding. It also provides a particularly provocative way to highlight the common-sense nature of that newness.

When I want to help a person address the progress question, I will often first engage them at a personal level. I will ask them to talk to me about what creates meaning—"wealth" in the largest sense—in their individual lives. Most people mention money, but they also tend to recognize that beyond a certain point, money stops being significant in the same sense. Invention, too, most always has a place—people like their gadgets. But most people appreciate that other things are ultimately as important—or often much more important: one's family, one's friends, one's community, one's felt relationship with nature, one's health, one's creative and intellectual pursuits.

People doing this exercise are often surprised to find that a significant mismatch exists between what they have described as most important for a meaningful life and many of their day-to-day choices. I may joke with the person as they confront this mismatch, pointing out—only partly tongue in cheek—that such discrepancy would seem to be almost the definition of insanity. When working in therapy, this kind of recognition can result in people making major life changes.

If the person has interest in the larger, cultural-level question, I may then engage them in the same kind of inquiry with regard to how collectively we define wealth and progress. People tend to come up with lists that are very similar, both in being more encompassing and in better reflecting basic needs. The fact that current world priorities reflect a related kind of mismatch becomes hard to escape. Too often today we apply an outmoded definition of advancement that excludes much that is in fact most important to us. And just as we appropriately think of individuals who make choices that are not in keeping with what they find most significant as deranged, the implications are huge. With the Dilemma of Trajectory, we see how continuing to take our Modern Age definition beyond its timeliness can only leave us distanced irreparably from much that most ultimately matters to us.

We will need more whole-box-of-crayons ways of defining progress not just if we are to usefully conceive of advancement as a whole, but also if we are to effectively engage almost any more specific critical task ahead for the species. Certainly, measures that follow from a more systemic definition will be required if we are to successfully assess the benefits and risks of new technologies. We need them if we are to effectively determine what we are to call benefit. Such measures will similarly be critical to making good environmental decisions. It is only through them that we can appreciate how impoverished further environmental destruction would leave us. And clearly a more mature and systemic definition for wealth and progress will be necessary if we are to effectively address the ever-widening gap between the world's haves and have-nots. Ask about benefit more consciously and we begin to better recognize not just how such disparities are ethically troubling, but how they risk destabilizing societies and putting everyone's well-being in peril.

It is important to appreciate how fundamentally different a culturally mature conception of wealth and progress is from more traditional definitions. This is the case in two essential ways. In contrast to Modern Age beliefs, it is more consciously arrived at. The old definition, like water for the proverbial fish, came inseparably with Modern Age assumptions. There is also how more systemic conceptions of advancement are more complete, both in terms of taking into account more factors and in more deeply drawing on the whole of who we are. In contrast, any kind of ideological belief, including beliefs of both the political right and the political left, identifies with particular crayons in cognition's whole-box-of-crayons complexity. Culturally mature measures, in drawing on the whole of our human complexity, step beyond simple-answer advocacies of all sorts. We come back to how Cultural Maturity's more complete picture is ultimately common sense. The measures that culturally mature perspective draws on simply ask us to be more fully attentive to all that matters to us.[8]

Cultural Maturity and the Long Term

I should note one further provocative implication of Cultural Maturity's cognitive changes. It concerns the concept's long-term significance. Cultural Maturity's most obvious importance lies with what it can tell us about the challenges we now face and the capacities required to meet them effectively. But the developmental interpretation that gives us the concept of Cultural Maturity supports an important additional recognition. Cultural Maturity may represent not just a new kind of narrative, it may provide at least a basic blueprint for understanding right thought and action well into humanity's future.

In times ahead, we should see changes that are products of technological advancement, certainly, but using technologies wisely will

---

8 We will examine this topic more conceptually in Chapter Five.

continue to require the general kind of perspective that Cultural Maturity's "growing up" as a species provides. And while we should see culturally mature perspective becoming ever more nuanced and detailed over time, the general cognitive architecture that generates it should continue to be the basis for needed understanding. It may well be that Cultural Maturity's changes mark not just the beginning of a needed next chapter in the human story, but the turning of first pages in a more encompassing kind of narrative that in the end will define our ultimate human task.

CHAPTER THREE

Creative Systems Theory's New Fundamental Organizing Concept— and the Power of Developmental Perspective

The insight that makes Creative Systems Theory's more detailed formulations wholly new is the power of a creative frame. I've described how thinking in creative terms provides a new Fundamental Organizing Concept able to take us beyond both machine-model notions of times past and romantic and idealist objections to such notions. It is a kind of recognition that becomes possible only with Cultural Maturity's cognitive changes. Indeed, we can think of a creative frame as following directly from them.

For example, we can arrive at a creative frame by considering how Integrative Meta-perspective "bridges" the polarized assumptions of times past. I've observed how polar relationships reflect an underlying symmetry. They juxtapose some harder, we could say more right-hand—or, to use the language from psychology, more archetypally masculine—quality with a quality that is softer, we could say more left-hand—or more archetypally feminine. There is an important sense in which the relationship between the two hands of any polarity, when understood systemically, becomes "procreative."

We get to a similar place if we shift our attention to intelligence. I've described how Integrative Meta-perspective makes it possible to better hold the whole of human intelligence. And I've proposed that intelligence's multiplicity functions to support and drive formative process. Integrative Meta-perspective, just from where it takes us, thrusts us into a world in which the workings of intelligence are dynamic and systemic, in a whole new sense—we could say, in a sense that is expressly creative.

The notion of a new kind of Fundamental Organizing Concept alters understanding regardless of what our concern is. And as with the cognitive reordering that makes the notion possible, there is no way to logically get there from how we have understood in times past. The notion reflects a leap in how we make sense of experience, one that could not be more profound in its implications.

Here I will address those implications from several different directions. I'll first draw on a particular notion from Creative Systems Theory—the Dilemma of Differentiation—to further fill out why this kind of leap is needed. The Dilemma of Differentiation clarifies how thinking in terms that reflect that we are living systems requires whole new kinds of concepts. It also helps us appreciate how a creative frame might provide a way to succeed at the task. I will then turn to how a creative frame lets us map change in human systems— what CST calls Patterning in Time. We got a start with Patterning in Time distinctions in the previous chapter with how we can see them reflected in the evolution of cultural narrative, in the stories we tell about how things work. With this chapter, I will come at Patterning in Time dynamics first by mapping the basic creative architecture that underlies human formative processes. We will then examine the radical recognition that we see this same basic creative patterning with human developmental processes of all sorts. Next, I will describe one particular dynamic reflected in this picture that helps distinguish it from ideas with which it might be confused. And I will conclude by reflecting on how Patterning in Time notions not only help us address the present and the future, they also fundamentally rewrite history.

Life and the Dilemma of Differentiation

I've pointed toward a question that brings immediate focus to the radical significance of a creative frame: How do we think in ways that honor the fact that we are alive? There is also a related more specific question: How do we think so that our ideas reflect the particular kind of life we are by virtue of being human? We confront the first question in the simple recognition that there is something obviously different between a rock and rhinoceros. And we face the second with how most people would agree that there is also something that separates ourselves and the creaturely (though we must keep in mind who is making this claim). Usual thinking leaves us at a loss to explain just what we see in either case.

As far as the life questions, if anyone should be an expert on life it would be a biologist. Yet if you ask biologists just what makes one thing alive and another not, and really push them on it, eventually they will just throw up their hands (or refer you to a philosopher, who will ultimately do no better[1]). And if you ask psychologists about just what makes us humans particular as creatures, they may point toward the fact of reflective awareness or make vague references to "consciousness."[2] But they will have little to offer that ultimately satisfies in terms of explaining the unique kind of vitality that comes with human life.

There is a further quandary embedded in these questions that takes on critical significance if our interest includes bringing any kind of detail to our thinking: How do we think about difference if our ideas are to honor the fact that we are alive (and, in particular, alive and human)? Creative Systems Theory calls this more specific quandary the Dilemma of Differentiation. Arguably, it is what in the end stops us in efforts to address the two more basic questions. The simple fact that culturally mature truth requires

---

1 Some philosophers might debate this assertion. But here my reference is to understanding that is able to get beyond the dualistic assumptions of times past. A philosopher might point to vitalists such as Henri Bergson who put the life question at the center of their considerations. But vitalism, in postulating a separate animating force (as with Bergson's "elan vital") is based on a dualistic premise. A philosopher might also go much further back and reference the ponderings of Aristotle. But with Aristotle's notion of an "unmoved mover," we again find a separate force necessarily to the fact of life.

2 I try to avoid using the word "consciousness" for reasons I will say more about in Chapter Seven. For now, it is enough to note that different ways that the term is used can suffer now-familiar polar fates. In the hands of cognitive science, ideas about consciousness tend to force-fit experience into mechanistic models. And in certain psychological circles, use of the term "consciousness" signals an identification with the spiritual. I will speak only of "conscious awareness" and use the phrase in a way that reflects that particular experience of awareness that comes with Integrative Meta-perspective.

that we make distinctions puts us immediately in a pickle. Differentiation, the ability to say "this as opposed to that," is ultimately what makes thinking work. But usual ways of addressing difference can't get us where we need to go if we want our ideas to reflect that we are living beings.

We find good illustration of this impasse in efforts to develop systemic approaches to understanding. Systems thinking emphasizes the importance of considering all the pieces involved in a process, that connections are as important as differences, and how in systems the whole ends up being greater than the sum of its parts. The importance of thinking systemically has become increasingly acknowledged over the last century, and systems ideas have been used in ways that have benefited us greatly. That importance should only increase in times to come.

But efforts to develop systems frameworks have consistently confronted the Dilemma of Differentiation. For example, the life question provided the inspiration for the pioneering work of Ludwig von Bertalanffy and his General Systems Theory. He made a good start at answering it. (In Chapter Seven I will say more about his approach.) But as far as his intended task of developing a comprehensive, detailed theory, the Dilemma of Differentiation stopped him from being successful in the way that he had hoped.[3]

Attempts to address difference tend to fall for one of two opposite kinds of traps. Both kinds of traps confront advocates of systemic thought. (Systemic understanding is unusual for the diverse—even opposite—worldviews that it can be used to justify.) The first kind of trap is most common. It confronts us with the same basic obstacle that we encounter with Modern Age thought more generally. A person depicts difference in traditional "parts"

---

3 I happily include Ludwig von Bertalanffy on my list of thinkers whose contributions get at least a toe over the threshold into culturally mature territory. But while he originally planned to develop a grand overarching scheme, he was never able to get beyond general principles. (Ludwig von Bertalanffy, *General Systems Theory*, George Braziller, 1968.) Systems thinkers who followed added detail by addressing strategies employed by life, such as feedback mechanisms. But in doing so, they reverted back to mechanistic models.

terms—that is, in an atomistic, mechanistic manner. The result may provide important detail. But no matter how subtle and sensitive the delineations, when the parts are put back together, we end up again in a machine world. Conventional systems ideas appreciate intricacies and interconnections, but even when the system of interest is a human body or an ecosystem teeming with organisms, the language stays that of a good engineer—hydraulics and forces, gears and pulleys. Such thinking fails to take into account the "living" nature of its subject.

Less common is an opposite, yet just as deadly, kind of trap. Many popular writers who use systems language—particularly writers of a more humanistic or spiritual bent—largely ignore parts and focus only on relationships. A frequent result is ideas that reduce to little more than elaborate ways of saying "all is one." Recognizing connectedness can be comforting—and it identifies a truth that is just as important and accurate as the "all is many" claims of atomistic or mechanistic belief. But slighting the significance of parts makes for impoverished conception at best. Worse, it makes for misleading conception. Real relationship (connectedness in the systemic sense this inquiry has interest in)—whether personal or conceptual—requires difference. Certainly life requires it.

A defining characteristic of culturally mature thought is that it succeeds in taking us beyond the Dilemma of Differentiation. We see hints at how it might in the way culturally mature understanding "bridges" conceptual polarities. We tend to associate polarity with opposed beliefs—such as the convictions of the political left set in contrast to those of the political right, or scientific assumptions juxtaposed with conclusions of a religious sort—but a more fundamental kind of polarity underlies all such more specific polar relationships. It is suggested in how polarities contrast archetypally masculine and archetypally feminine qualities. The most basic of polarities juxtaposes difference and multiplicity on one hand with connectedness and oneness on the other. (Note the critical implication that when we identify with oneness we are quite specifically taking sides.) "Bridging" of this ultimate polarity is implied whenever any more specific bridging comes into play. One result is that any notion that draws a circle around traditional conceptual polarities—and really does so—will take us beyond the limited viewpoints of both mechanistic and unitary formulations.

A good way to recognize the radical implications of Creative Systems Theory's contribution is to appreciate the fact that a creative frame, just by its nature, reconciles the Dilemma of Differentiation. Creative understanding, whatever our concern, "bridges" more right-hand and more left-hand sensibilities. In the process, it allows us to make highly detailed distinctions and have our identification of difference increase, rather than diminish, our appreciation for the dynamic nature of life. We find a third option beyond mechanistic difference and the unitary in all creatively framed concepts.

A creative frame is not the only way to address the Dilemma of Differentiation, but arguably it has particular significance. At least with regard to human life, it provides something quite precise. I've described the challenge of culturally mature systemic perspective as thinking in ways that reflect not just that we are alive, but also alive in the particular ways that make us human. If what most makes us human is our striking toolmaking—creative—capacities, then a creative frame should have particular utility and precision when the concern is ourselves.[4]

Can we extend this observation further? Do we appropriately think of biological life and existence as a whole as ultimately creative? In a sense, perhaps (a topic that I will return to in Chapter Seven). But such conclusions leave us very close to common conceptual traps. Certainly we must take care that we don't simply project our time's new cognitive mechanisms as Enlightenment perspective did in assuming a mechanical universe. It is better that we say simply that whatever strategy we apply, it has to accomplish results similar to what is accomplished with a creative frame.

---

4 We find important thinkers historically who anticipated the application of a creative frame. I think in particular of Alfred North Whitehead. In his major work, *Process and Reality*, he described creativity as "the universal of universals." But as with how early systems thinking could provide only a general approach, Whitehead was never able to get beyond the articulation of general principles. (Alfred North Whitehead, *Process and Reality*, Simon and Schuster, 2010.)

Patterning in Time

Creative Systems Theory includes three kinds of differentiating notions, what it speaks of as "patterning concepts:" Patterning in Time, Whole-Person/Whole-System patterning concepts, and Patterning in Space. Each, by applying a creative frame, reconciles the Dilemma of Differentiation. Patterning in Time, the topic of this chapter, is concerned with change and human development. Whole-Person/Whole-System patterning notions, a topic in Chapter Five, address questions related to truth at its most basic, purpose, and capacity. And Patterning in Space concepts, a topic in Chapter Six, address here-and-now human differences—for example, personality style diversity.

Patterning in Time notions have most immediate pertinence to this book's reflections when it comes to understanding how cultural systems change over time. Creative Systems Theory maps how cultural change has identifiable stages. And it highlights how those stages reflect a more general kind of creative architecture. I've observed how ideas that view culture as evolving tend to be immediately suspect in certain circles and noted the common explanation that they can be misused to justify bigoted interpretations.[5] The important recognition for these reflections is that Cultural Maturity's changes put such objections in the past. Without Integrative Meta-perspective, evolutionary pictures of history are indeed vulnerable to abuse. But with it, for the first time we get a picture that begins to capture what is unique, rich, and powerful with each chapter of our human story.

The fact that cultures evolve in ways that have identifiable stages is really quite obvious with reflection. We find good illustration in how spiritual/religious understanding has taken different forms at various

---

5 I've also noted that this is likely only part of the reason such thinking tends to be dismissed. I suspect such dismissal has as much to do with how today's postmodern climate makes any kind of deep distinction taboo. And more deeply, there is how any view of the past that effectively grasps the significance of earlier cultural realities requires us to draw on the whole of intelligence's multiplicity. In Chapter Six I will describe how we find a similar kind of hesitancy in academia with regard to Patterning in Space distinctions such as personality style differences. I suspect this is for related reasons.

times. In tribal times, the spiritual was animistic, with the sacred manifesting as creatures and places. Next we find more polytheistic belief, as with Olympian Greece, ancient Egypt, or the many gods of Hindu practice. This was followed by monotheistic forms, first of a more fundamentalist sort with medieval belief, and later with modern times, forms that were more liberal and less severe. We can find a related kind of progression if we turn to any kind of belief or activity—scientific, governmental, philosophical, or artistic. Creative Systems Theory not only maps this kind of progression, it describes how it is predicted given how developmental processes in human systems work. It also predicts that with Cultural Maturity's changes we should find ourselves capable of more encompassing conception. Such conception appreciates how the realities of each stage are "true" in their time. It also appreciates how we might in our time be able to entertain more encompassing and complete possibilities.

To understand Patterning in Time, it helps to start with a closer look at creative patterning at its most basic. I've described how insights that followed from delving into the workings of creative process provided some of my first and most foundational insights. In beginning my inquiry into creative process, I expected that the topic had been studied and written about extensively. I found that it had not, for reasons that only became clear over time (and that with time similarly helped me understand how academic thought was rarely going to be as helpful as I might hope when it came to culturally mature understanding). So I dove in to see what I could usefully discern on my own.

The first insights related to formative process most generally. I've proposed that Creative Systems Theory provides an answer to the question of why we think in polar terms in the first place. It describes how the fact that historically we have thought in the language of polarity follows from our creative, toolmaking, meaning-making natures. The theory delineates how the generation of polarity is necessary to formative process. Formative processes of all sorts reflect a related architecture. The first half of any formative process brings the newly created object or idea into being and in the process generates polarity. The second half reintegrates that which has now been made manifest with the context from which it originated, and in so doing establishes a new, now expanded whole.

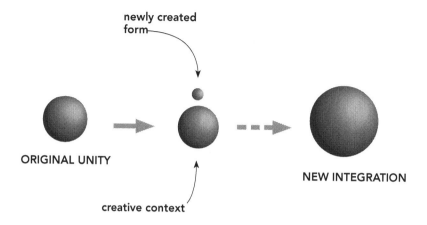

Fig. 3-1. Differentiation and New Integration in Creative/Formative Process

If we wish to think with greater detail, we can take this simple picture of polarity's generative workings and extend it like the bellows of an accordion. The first half of formative process then becomes an evolving play of polarities, with polarity in each stage following a predictable progression. Creative Systems Theory describes the first half of any human formative process as having incubation, inspiration, perspiration, and finishing and polishing stages. The juxtapositions of each succeeding stage reflect greater identification with the newly created form and diminishing identification with the context from which it originates.

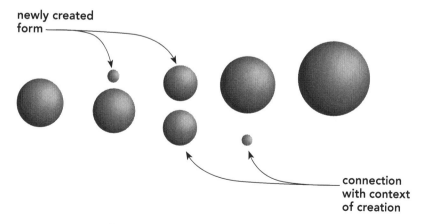

Fig. 3-2. Polarity's Evolution Over the First Half of Formative Process

When we include the second half of formative process, we get a template for understanding formative process wherever we might find it. Creative Systems Theory calls this generic map, applicable to formative dynamics from the most personal of insights to the most encompassing of collective processes, the Creative Function.

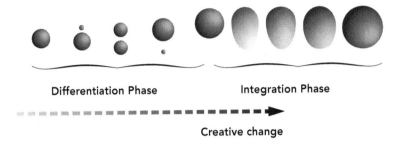

Fig. 3-3. The Creative Function

We can recognize this two-part extended picture in personal psychological development. I've noted how the underlying impetus with development in the first half of an individual life is toward distinction and the establishing of identity as form. With childhood we begin discovering who we are, with adolescence we make our first forays into the social world, and during adulthood we establish our unique place in that world. And I've described how second-half-of-life maturing involves more specifically integrative tasks. It is about learning how to live in the world with the greatest perspective, depth, and integrity.

The Creative Function presents a simplified picture. Stages can vary in length and emphasis depending on the kind of system and surrounding circumstances. And formative processes can be aborted at any stage. But the general sequence holds with remarkable consistency. For our purposes, the important recognition is that it holds as predictably at a cultural scale as it does for more circumscribed formative processes such as creating a work of art or the evolving play of interactions that produce a relationship. It also strongly supports Cultural Maturity's conclusions.

Patterning in Time Applied

The recognition that we find this same basic progression underlying change processes in human systems of all sorts—from simple creative acts, to individual psychological development, to the development of relationships, to the evolution of cultural systems—is radical and for most people rather startling. It was for me. I could have stopped with the basic notion of creative organization and at least made a contribution to understanding our dramatically inventive natures. With the recognition of developmental parallels, we get something more that gives Creative Systems Theory much of both its radical significance and its practical importance. Again, it is a kind of recognition that becomes possible only with Integrative Meta-perspective.

I've promised with this book to focus on documenting examples of radical newness and leave more extended descriptions to other resources. But because of the importance of these parallels both for understanding the power of a creative frame and for the practical application of Creative Systems ideas, I will address them in a more extended fashion. And in keeping with the primary task with this volume, I will give cultural dynamics particular attention.

These reflections are adapted from my book *Creative Systems Theory*. The theory has more formal language for what I've described as the incubation, inspiration, perspiration, and finishing and polishing stages. It calls them Pre-Axis, Early-Axis, Middle-Axis, and Late-Axis respectively. I include this more formal language here as it will help avoid confusion when addressing questions of contextual relativity more broadly in Chapter Six. I've chosen working on a piece of sculpture (where much of my early artistic attention focused) to make the simple creative act more vivid.

Creative "Incubation" (Pre-Axis):

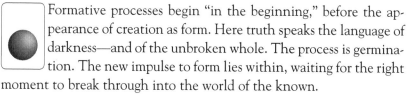

Formative processes begin "in the beginning," before the appearance of creation as form. Here truth speaks the language of darkness—and of the unbroken whole. The process is germination. The new impulse to form lies within, waiting for the right moment to break through into the world of the known.

In a simple creative act, like my working on a piece of sculpture, this is the incubation stage. I may have a vague sense that something is preparing to happen, but nothing is yet visible. If I'm sensitive, I can feel some of the primordial beginnings in my tissues—perhaps in an attraction to a certain kind of movement, a feeling of contained shape, a gentle expanding.

In a lifetime, this is the prenatal period and the first few months of life. The unbroken whole speaks in the infant's relationship both to the mother and to itself. Even following birth, the bond to the mother is what is primary. The light of conscious volition, that evidence of first distinction of both self from self and self from other, is only preparing to awaken. The reality of the infant is an unselfconscious creature world. To feel is to act; there is no separation.

In a new relationship, this is the time before there is anything really visible as relationship. I may have a sense of being open to the possibility for a new connecting. I may have even met the person and felt a certain "chemistry" in her presence. But the spark of conscious recognition has yet to ignite.

In the story of civilization, this incubation stage corresponds to Stone Age times. For the most part, this is a reality of our distant past, though there are still a few places on our planet—in the New Guinea highlands, the upper Amazon basin, some places in the Australian outback—where this primordial reality can prevail. The unbroken whole at a cultural scale is multilayered, at once the tribe, nature, and time. In early tribal realities, the "body" of the tribe is more accurately the primary organism than the individuals who compose it. At once, truth and nature exist as, in essence, a single thing. Tribal deities are simply the faces of nature set animate: the wind, the mountain, bear, eagle, coyote. Health is one's degree of harmony with this living nature. Knowing is one's bodily connection in and as this whole. And time similarly affirms this unbroken entirety. Existence takes place in an eternally cycling present. Each generation and each turning of the seasons reenacts a timeless story.

Creative "Inspiration" (Early-Axis):

The next big slice makes the magic and numinosity of the creative most explicit. Newly created possibility now steps forth from mystery into the light. This dramatic movement fundamentally alters how we perceive the order of things. Truth becomes explicitly polar. And its primary mode of expression shifts from the kinesthetic to the symbolic, to the language of myth and metaphor.

In working with chisel and stone, this is the stage of first insight. What was before only a faint quickening is now visibly born. My task is to play with images and possibilities, to feel where in them the deepest power lies, and to risk giving that power first form.

In a lifetime, this is the magical world of childhood. In this stage, we see the first critical distinction in initial separation from mother and, in first manifestations of individual awareness, separation from the infant's more creature-like reality. Truth moves a bit more "into the light," organized now according to the laws of imagination. The critical work of the child is its play, trying out images of possibility on the stage of make-believe and let's pretend.

With intimacy, this part of the story has its beginning with the first blush of real attraction. It's a magical time, filled with tentative first touchings and fantasies of the possible. We are still largely strangers, and our connecting is often more as numinous symbols than as simple mortals ... a fair princess, a handsome prince.

With the story of civilization, this stage takes us to the time of early civilizations. It first manifests in the coming together of tribes into broader allegiances. It reaches its full splendor with the classical high cultures—in the mystical monumentality of ancient Egypt, the vibrant artistry of pre-Columbian Mesoamerica, or the great mythic tales of Olympian Greece and the rich philosophies that followed. But we can also find current examples of this inspiration stage in culture—in places like Tibet (though Chinese occupation has tempered the inspiration) or Bali (though more so prior to the tourist invasion). This is the time of culture's initial flowerings. Something more than just nature (spirit, essence, magic, beauty—no single word quite does it) emerges as the new cultural referent in these times. It manifests with particular directness in myth, speaking through epic tales and complex pantheons of major and minor gods. This is also a time of rich artistic potency. Art during this stage becomes not just expression, but in and of itself, a form of truth. We also see philosophy's inspired beginnings.

Creative "Perspiration"(Middle-Axis):

Creation's perspiration stage takes the possible into solid form. It galvanizes the conviction, focus, and endurance that concrete manifestation requires. With the beginnings of this stage, we may easily feel that something is being lost. The preceding stage was magical and numinous. Now the predominant feelings are often hard work and struggle. But this stage is in no way less significant—and no less creative. The moment of first inspiration is indeed wondrous, but it is only a first step on the road to fully realized creation. With creative perspiration the language of truth shifts from the mythic to the moral and the emotional. The work progresses by virtue of heart and guts. We can understand why this experience of struggle might be common by looking at the underlying polar dynamics. By the middle of this stage, the power of the newly created and the power of the context of creation have become equivalent. Reality exists as a polar isometric between at once opposite and conspiring forces.

As a sculptor, it is here that I most directly grapple with the hard demands of my calling. I must confront both the brute fact of the stone and my own limitations. Sometimes work proceeds with the patient rhythms and quiet satisfactions of the craftsman. Other times I rage. Over the course of this stage my relationship to the work changes, becoming both more vigorous and more expressive of the work as a human act.

In a lifetime, this stage bids entry into adolescence. Adolescence is a heroic time, but also often an awkward and troubled time. The innocence of childhood must be left behind. It's a time for us to heroically challenge external limits and establish inner ones. Emotions can be strong and contradictory. The reward for perseverance is an increasingly established identity and successful preparation for entry into the adult world.

With love, this stage engages us in the tasks of relationship building. The challenges can be immensely satisfying—coming to better know the other person's gifts and peculiarities, beginning to craft a life together. And again we commonly find contradictory feelings. The glow of the honeymoon period—with the other as dream image—necessarily fades. This is the stage at which we most directly deal with questions of control and territory. It's here we decide who takes out the garbage.

This stage in cultural dynamics ruled in the West from the time of the Roman Empire through the Middle Ages and predominates today in much of the Middle East, as well as playing a key role in parts of Eastern Europe, Southeast Asia, and Central and South America. We find great wonders, from the Roman aqueducts to Europe's monumental

Gothic cathedrals. And equally we find struggle (and not infrequently pain and inhumanity)—the Crusades and the Spanish Inquisition, the European Dark Ages, and, in more modern times, often intractable conflict and the tyranny of brutal dictatorships. The emotional and moral assume new prominence at this stage. Beliefs commonly reflect a fundamentalist ardency, and a newly equal, and frequently ambivalent, balance between polar forces orders cultural experience. The European Middle Ages saw social structures become increasingly feudal, landed lords above, serfs and the otherwise impoverished below; church and state (here in the form of kingly rule) become newly separate, newly equal, and ever-more-frequently at odds; and the ancients' many gods with their differing proclivities surrendering their power to the notion of a single deity—or more accurately a dual deity—a monotheistic godhead in eternal battle with the forces of evil. In the modern world, one of the easiest ways to find perspiration stage cultural sensibilities is to note where conflict is common and particularly intractable. Again, we might regret that a certain magic has been lost. But this is not regression. The reward for this loss is increasingly established social structure. The Middle Ages gave us, with kingly rule, a new solidification of social organization, establishment of an institutional church, radical validation of rights with the Magna Carta, and increasingly formal structures of communication and commerce. We find related advances—and related contradictions—wherever perspiration stage developmental realities dominate in contemporary times.

Creative "Finishing and Polishing" (Late-Axis):

Our progression has thus far taken us from the mystery of the formless into magical possibility and first form, and then through a time of solidification of form. New form now gets its finishing touches. Attention shifts increasingly to refinement and detail. Poles become even more separate, giving reality two nearly distinct faces. Truth becomes increasingly rational and material, defined in terms of logic and phenomena that can be seen and measured. And, at the same time, it becomes newly personal and subjective— the truth of aesthetics and even whim.

At this stage, as I face that piece of stone, I become newly able to objectively step back. The work now sits before me as a "piece," ready for completion. My focus shifts increasingly to issues of detail, to making sure that all the elements are there and fit correctly together, to questions of aesthetic refinement and final nuance. And audience comes to have increasing importance. I need to give the newly created piece the clarity of delineation necessary if it is to communicate effectively.

In personal development, it is here that we face the tasks of adulthood. Adulthood challenges us to refine identity, to make essential decisions regarding career and family, and to give nuance and detail—and one's personal stamp—to the way we live our lives. More than at any other time, identity can be described in terms of things we can objectively see and measure—the structures we have given our lives and the forms of our actions. Adulthood is the most explicitly "in the world" stage of life.

Love at this stage becomes established and defined. We've sorted out the major issues of being together and reached general agreement on the roles and boundaries of relationship—who does what, how, and when. We've largely stopped asking what our relationship will be, because it now is. Our attention shifts to details and fine-tuning. If we've chosen to continue together, love's connection at this point frequently has a feeling of calm and acceptance not present in earlier stages.

In the story of civilization, this is the Modern Age, the last four hundred years in Western Europe and at least an ingredient in the sensibilities of most cultural systems today. If classical times marked Europe's childhood, and the medieval period its adolescence, modernity marked its coming of age. As culture engages finishing and polishing dynamics, oral and kingly truths give way to more materially ordered realities—a personal reality of individuality, intellect, and achievement; a social reality of law, industry, and economics; and a physical reality of actions and their concomitant reactions. Institutions come to reflect a new appreciation for individual freedom and individual initiative. Governmental forms begin to become representative; religion entertains newly personal and direct relationships with the divine; and economic competition becomes its own ethic, freeing business from moral constraint. With the Modern Age in Europe we witnessed the Age of Reason and the growing prominence of science with its new emphasis on the empirical. We also witnessed reason's counterbalance in the Romantic

Age, with its emphasis on nature and the artistic. At this stage a sense of impending completion permeates culture. People speak of it being only a matter of time until all of life's great mysteries find elucidation and individual freedom is fully realized.[6]

Transition and Creative Integration

I've made reference to Transitional dynamics as they pertain to cultural systems. And I've introduced the related Dilemma of Trajectory and the concept of Transitional Absurdity. Examining Transition's more general role in formative process helps clarify its significance.

Part of the "finishing and polishing" stage story is that we have reached completion. The piece of sculpture is done. Identity is established. The hard work of relationship is over. We have brought understanding into the full light of reason. But polarity has in fact told but half of its story. Much that is most important in the "respiration" of creative life has yet to take place. And it is a good thing that this is so. It is these additional creative stages, and the additional kind of polar relationships they involve, that make Cultural Maturity possible. I've described how formative processes have two halves. Polarity has very different significance depending on which half we inhabit.

To appreciate how this is so, and before that, what just getting to such second-half realities requires, we need first to add an additional stage—or more accurately, a time between stages. I've introduced how it has particular importance for understanding these formative times in culture.

---

6 A number of important thinkers have observed more limited parallels between individual psychological development and culture's evolution. For example, Eric Neumann, drawing on initial insights from Jung, did so through the comparative study of mythology and individual symbolism in *The Origins and History of Consciousness* (Bollingen, 1954). Philosopher Jürgen Habermas observed a connection drawing on Lawrence Kohlberg's theory of moral development (with its roots in the thinking of Jean Piaget). And existential psychologist Eric Fromm suggested a similar kind of relationship in his book *The Sane Society* (Henry Holt, 1955). CST's formulations are more encompassing in addressing formative process wherever we find it. They also provide explanation for just why we see the parallels that we do that are not found with other formulations.

Creative "Transition":

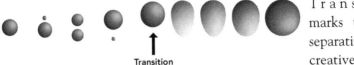

Transition marks the line separating the creative jour-ney's two halves. I've pointed toward how Transitional changes are different from earlier developmental leaps in that they involve more than letting go of one stage and moving to another. In the end, they bring into question the entire developmental orientation (toward ever greater ascendancy, separation, and solidification of form) that has defined growth and truth. Transition can be a profound time—in its confrontations lie the seeds of real maturity and even wisdom. But it is also a time of disorientation and inescapable uncertainty. We stand at a precipice. Do we leap and trust that solid ground is to be found? Do we go back? Proceeding depends on the gradual discovery of a new completeness in how we relate to both ourselves and our world. Transition is creation's continental divide.

The piece of sculpture is done. It stands before me as a crowning achievement. But what now? During the process of its creation I have come to be almost more the sculpture than myself. And now, suddenly, I must let it go. I could be tempted out of fear to cling to the piece, refuse its surrender. But if I do that, the piece becomes increasingly tired and purposeless, and I myself become increasingly absurd. I could just blindly walk away. But where do I go—indeed, is there any place to go?

With individual development we confront the unique and unexpected challenges of midlife. Just as we thought we were done, the most fundamental of questions reappear and block our way. In time, this necessary questioning touches every part of our lives—our work, our love, and ultimately our most basic ideas about who we are and how the world functions. The sense of purpose that we once took for granted can feel suddenly elusive. We ask, So who am I, really? And what really matters to me? At this point we have no way of knowing whether anything lies ahead—at least anything that can excite. Perhaps the future promises only being over the hill. Some people respond to this uncertainty by abandoning what they have been—by getting a divorce, leaving their jobs. Others cling to old beliefs or try to return to their youth. But we have no real choice but to live with the uncertainty. When we attempt to hide from it, perversely, we only feel more empty and confused.

We see something similar with the midpoint in love as a creative process. Suddenly, just as we thought our work done, the passions that have driven love can elude us. The same sense of completion that before gave us pride easily begins to feel like habit, and the comfort of familiarity easily feels like taking each other for granted. We have become for each other all-too-familiar objects. Where to go from here? Stepping forward requires that we surrender that familiarity, and with it our dreams of perfection and completion. But is there anything beyond these things? We have no way to know. In fear, we often cling to what we know. But when we do, our relationship becomes empty and stale.

Creative Systems Theory proposes that much of what we see today culturally has its origins in Transitional dynamics. As a species, we stand at a precipice. Old answers are ceasing to work and, by all evidence, they will not be replaced by new ones, at least not of the same sort. What lies ahead? Anything? From the apex of Transition we cannot know. We can try to cling to familiar truths—from the onward-and-upward story of material progress to religious predictions of final salvation or damnation. But when we do, we only become more absurd. I've touched on how postmodern thought gives voice to the Transitional predicament. Postmodern social formulations such as those of existentialism and social constructivism have emphasized the diminishing usefulness of final truths of every sort—truths based on cultural belief. I've also described how even the best of such notions can only get us part of the way. They may eloquently address the Transitional quandary, but by themselves they give us no way to understand whether anything of real substance lies beyond it.

With Transition we reside at a threshold, at a doorway joining two related but also fundamentally different worlds. The Transitional quandary at a cultural level today often takes some particularly troubling forms, what I've referred to as Transitional Absurdity. Some Transitional Absurdities simply reflect that this can be an awkward in-between time. Others reflect how much Transitional dynamics stretch us beyond what we easily tolerate. Whatever their source, moving forward hinges on our ability to bring Cultural Maturity's more systemic picture to bear.

Creative "Integration":

Stepping over maturity's threshold—whatever the creative scale—offers that we might leave Transition's precarious reality behind us. We are necessarily surprised by what we encounter—surprised that so much of creation's journey remains ahead, at the magnitude of what it will ask of us, and at the depth and richness of its potential rewards. Transition in one sense marks a completion, in another a beginning—of a systemically mature creative life. While we may have thought creation finished, or nearly so, in fact we have barely approached its midpoint. Yes, the new object of creation (the piece of sculpture, personal identity, relationship as an entity, or culture as structure) stands shining before us. But it has yet to be significantly tested. Integration is about that testing—and the creative changes that result, not just in that object, but also in everything that surrounds it.

The second half of the creative cycle reconnects the new creation with the personal and social contexts from which it was born. It is about bringing maturity to the creative process. We become newly able to step back from the whole of the creative mechanism, and, with this, to better appreciate where it has taken us and what ultimately it has been about. A word like "integration" comes close to describing what takes place, but this is not integration in any simple additive or oneness-generating sense. The changes that take place in these integrative stages are as fully creative as any seen before. They change everything—fundamentally.

Key to what we see is how Integration provides perspective of a newly encompassing sort, what I've pointed toward with the concept of Integrative Meta-perspective. Integrative Meta-perspective dramatically changes how we see the world—and ourselves. Our interest becomes increasingly not just the newly created object, but that object in living relationship with all that surrounds it. We also better appreciate the degree in which *how* we perceive affects *what* we perceive. And we better recognize how truths that before seemed separate or even adversarial—many of which are essential to our sense of identity—may work as colluding partners.

Before this developmental point, such changes would have seemed only disorienting and overwhelming. As Integration Phase dynamics become timely, we experience them as positive. They make possible a sophistication of understanding—and of life—that we could not have known before. Within the limits of any formative process's particular creative scale, we engage a more conscious and explicitly complex, whole-box-of-crayons world of experience.

As I step back from that piece of stone and examine the finished sculpture it has now become, I confront how the journey of its creation is in fact far from over. The piece may need further seasoning, and, even if not, it has yet to be placed in the world. What will happen to it? Will it make the world a better place, be ignored, be destroyed? And in an important sense, it has also yet to be placed in me. Much remains to happen. On "completing" a piece of real significance, it is often years before I can say with any clarity what it is really about, what it has to teach. The conscious object of creation before was the stone. Creative maturity reveals that my engagement with it has always been as much about creating myself, and, if it truly functions as art, about new possibilities in the creation of culture.

The primary achievements of the first half of development in our individual lives—self-definition, the acquisition of skills and knowledge, perhaps creating a family—are all in some way concerned with establishing ourselves as form. The developmental challenges of life's second half make real in ever-more-subtle ways the fact that creative Transition first made inescapable—that the role of such forms in the tasks of truth and identity is but a beginning. Truth as answer increasingly gives way to truth as perspective and interrelationship. Questions present themselves that can't be answered in the old ways, questions of a newly contextual sort. We reexamine our professions, looking to see if they still provide challenge and fulfillment in our lives—and, as important, if they contribute in satisfying ways. We do the same with our relationships and our beliefs. In the process, who we are in each of these spheres deepens. Frequently our choices remain largely as before—it is primarily our relationship to our choices that changes. But sometimes too we make new choices, venture off in wholly new directions. Questions of perspective and meaning increasingly move forefront. When we say someone is mature, seasoned, or wise, we appreciate that they have engaged and weathered at least the most important of life's Integrative challenges.

Love's second-half dynamics give new emphasis to the uniqueness of each person and to the unique needs of the relationship. Bonds become at once richer and more humble. When we are more fully ourselves, our connection can deepen. But this can happen only with the acceptance of limits to what one person can be for another. Being together with fullness and honesty—however that might look—increasingly defines affection and commitment. We more deeply appreciate self and other as particular and complex beings.

Central to Cultural Maturity's argument is the recognition that societal circumstances increasingly demand the more fully encompassing kind of cognitive perspective we would expect second-half creative dynamics at a cultural scale to involve. I've described how both the objectivist/rationalist/materialist/individualist truths that have dominated our most recent stage in culture and more romantic and idealist reactions to them are insufficient for addressing the tasks before us. We confront challenges in every sphere that require that we abandon polar ideologies and assumptions and think in more complete and embracing ways. And tasks of every sort are presenting us with fundamental questions of context and meaning. More and more, we must make conscious choices in a newly complex, often uncertain, deeply interconnected, and ever-evolving world. We are being challenged in our time to become, in ways not before conceivable, consciously responsible, mature choice-makers in the larger human story.

Even without potentially cataclysmic Transitional Absurdities, these circumstances can seem precarious. We could easily imagine that our times mark the end of civilization. In the sense of confronting Transition's threshold, they do mark an end. Our times mark the end of a way of organizing experience and making sense of ourselves that in its general contours has been with us since our species's beginnings. From the near side of that threshold there is no way to know whether anything lies beyond what we see, and every reason to assume we will find only problems ahead. But a step over maturity's threshold reveals that a great deal potentially lies before us. We can't know all the specifics or whether we can pull off what the future will require. But this developmental picture makes strong argument for the conclusion that the rewards for venturing forth could very well be not just exciting, but of essential significance.

CREATIVE STAGES

	Pre-Axis	Early-Axis	Middle-Axis	Late-Axis	Transition	Integrative Stages
A CREATIVE EVENT	Incubation	Inspiration	Perspiration	Finishing & Polishing	Presentation	Becoming "Second Nature" (Integration of the newly created form into self and culture)
A LIFETIME	Prenatal Period & Infancy	Childhood	Adolescence	Early Adulthood	Midlife Transition	Mature Adulthood (From knowledge to wisdom—integration of self as formed identity with the ground of being)
A RELATIONSHIP	Pre-relationship	Falling in Love	Time of Struggle	Established Relationship	Time of Questioning	Mature Intimacy (Relationship as two whole people—marriage of the "loved" and the "lover" within each person)
THE HISTORY OF CULTURE	Pre-History	Golden Ages	Middle Ages	Age of Reason	Transitional Culture	Cultural Maturity (Larger meeting of the form and context of culture)

MAJOR PERIODICITIES

Fig. 3-4. The Creative Function with Major Formative Periodicities

Developmental Amnesias and Reengagement

These descriptions take us beyond more familiar ways of thinking about change in human systems. Certainly they leave behind views that see change only in terms of rational problem solving, will, or invention—with regard to culture, the kind that produces familiar onward-and-upward images of progress. And just as much, they leave behind more romantic or spiritual formulations. They reveal these historical viewpoints to be each in its own way ideological, and a way of thinking that leaves us fundamentally short of the kind of fully systemic understanding that times ahead will require.

We need a further kind of insight if this developmental picture is to be complete and effectively guide us in our time. It involves the mechanism that Creative Systems Theory calls Reengagement. We need the concept of Reengagement if either the implications of Integrative Meta-perspective or the appropriateness of a creative frame as a basis for understanding developmental processes and the tasks ahead for the species is to make full sense.

Culturally mature perspective's picture of the future takes us unswervingly forward, but at the same time it implies something new with regard to the past. It does more than just help us better understand the past, though there is that. It invites—indeed requires—a deeper connection with the past—or, more accurately, with aspects of ourselves to which we have had more ready access in times past. Reengagement has been implied in how I've spoken of culturally mature understanding in terms of a more encompassing relationship with intelligence's multiplicity. Along with helping clarify how Integrative Meta-perspective produces the results I have described, the concept of Reengagement also helps us distinguish Cultural Maturity from other ways of thinking about the challenges before us. There are other frameworks that suggest something that might seem similar, but none that I am aware of that capture all that is involved and get us to quite the same place.

A further insight beyond the basic notion is needed if the concept of Reengagement is to be fully grasped. It has to do with how developmental leaps between one stage and another, along with offering new possibilities, also involve necessary forgettings—amnesias for realities we've moved beyond. Personal development highlights this dynamic. Adolescents, we find, have a difficult time making sense of the reality of young children even though this is a world that they have only recently left behind. And while we might expect young adults to be our great experts on the attitudes and needs of adolescence, it is often they who find adolescent assumptions most baffling. With each organizational leap, doors close to past experience.

People can find the idea that development involves amnesias strange, but at some level we all know this is how things work. Children universally believe in Santa Claus and the Easter Bunny (or their culture's equivalents). And most adults think of such figures as fantasy at best. Yet few parents try to convince their children of the irrationality of such belief. In some way parents know that such "illusion" is essential to being children. More, they recognize at some level that something very special lives in this illusion that they can only faintly recollect. Its elusive presence is much of what makes such childhood delight special to adults.

Developmental amnesias in our individual lives distance us from more than just memories. They disconnect us from the organizing sensibilities of the realities we have left behind and the values and ways of seeing the world that accompany previous stages. With each developmental chapter we distance ourselves from fundamental dimensions of our being. Such forgetting serves a critical developmental purpose. It keeps us from falling back into familiar but no longer timely worlds of experience. Growing up requires not just separation from family as home, but also separation from the ways of organizing experience that at different, earlier times have served as our cognitive/experiential homes.

With development in the second half of life, we witness an almost opposite mechanism—a kind of anamnesis. Once the basic structures of identity and belief have been established, the protective doors provided by these developmental amnesias can begin to reopen. We no longer need to fear the past. Memories from earlier times in life often become newly available. And of ultimately greater significance, second-half-of-life maturity bit by bit reconnects us with those earlier ordering principles—the intelligences, values, aesthetics, and creative juxtapositions that have given previous developmental stages their unique character and power. We reengage forgotten dimensions of who we are.

This dual mechanism—first necessary forgetting, then a later remembering—is something we see with human generative processes of every sort. Amnesias serve like cogs so the wheels of life do not turn backward during creativity's fragile early stages. Once form is sufficiently established, the past stops being something to fear. It becomes instead a necessary part of mature understanding's larger, more complete picture.

We should expect each of these dynamics to manifest in a similar way with culture's developmental story. Certainly the idea of developmental amnesias is consistent with what we have witnessed historically. I think of developmental amnesias playing a central role in how in times past we have viewed cultural stages previous to our own. Combine developmental amnesias with our past tendency to project aspects of our systemic complexity onto peoples different from ourselves, and it is not surprising that historically we have commonly viewed the cultural practices of times past in distorted ways. Looking to the future, we should find Reengagement's integrative mechanisms altering both how we understand ourselves and how we view previous cultural realities. Grasping the multiplicities and coherences of our deep systemic natures should provide not just an appreciation of current complexities, but also a deeper understanding of—and connection with—human complexity through time.

Reengagement at a cultural level produces a result that we have not before seen when it comes to the realities of previous cultural times. With Cultural Maturity's cognitive reordering, we step fully beyond what has been, but at the same time we find a new and deeper connection with the sensibilities that past stages reflect. We can appreciate this essential distinction in how culturally mature perspective engages history's most recent truths. Rather than discarding the objectivist/rationalist/materialist/individualist assumptions of Modern Age belief as we have done previously with the assumptions of past cultural times, Cultural Maturity makes them part of complexity's now expanded picture. Cultural Maturity does something similar with regard to other even earlier cultural realities. I've described Cultural Maturity's cognitive reordering in terms of the "bridging" of polarities. We can think of the result with Reengagement as a kind of temporal "bridging."

The concept of Reengagement can cause initial confusion and is easily misinterpreted. For example, on first encounter people can assume that Reengagement in some way involves resurrecting the past. In fact, it is not even about reconnecting with the past. What we "reengage" is forgotten sensibilities as they exist in the present. But once understood, the concept provides important insight into how Cultural Maturity changes the way we think and act. None of Cultural Maturity's key concepts make full sense without this additional mechanism.

We find an everyday sort of support for Reengagement in the way people who spend much time in settings that are not yet modern quickly recognize that much—and much of real significance—has been lost as well as gained in the phenomenon we call progress. There are clearly qualities and affinities present in these earlier realities that are not only important, but somehow essential to recapture if our future world is to be a healthy place. Few people remain happy for long if plunked down in a cultural reality earlier than their own. But it becomes clear that sensibilities before forgotten—and forgotten for good reasons—in fact have importance.

One major consequence of Reengagement is that in a further way it supports the idea that a positive human future might be an option. When we have a deeper appreciation for aspects of experience more deeply valued in times past, in an important further way the Dilemma of Trajectory stops being a dilemma. The more complete picture that becomes visible with Reengagement offers an essential option beyond going forward as we have, going back, or collapse. That new possibilities might exist beyond what had seemed an ultimate obstacle begins to make better sense. It becomes not just reasonable, but predicted, that we might be able to "progress" in ways specifically right for our time.

The concept of Reengagement provides an important compare-and-contrast tool for distinguishing Cultural Maturity from other ways of thinking about humanity's future. Certainly it suggests a different kind of outcome than either We've Arrived or onward-and-upward utopian views. And just as much it highlights the inadequacy of views that in some way idealize the beliefs of times past and suggest that such beliefs should serve as our answers going forward. It also presents a picture that is fundamentally different from what we more often find with evolutionary interpretations. More commonly with such views, each stage is thought to at once advance beyond and incorporate the realities of previous stages. An appreciation for both developmental amnesias and the specific kind of anamnesis that we find with Reengagement is needed if we are to fully grasp either the implications of Integrative Meta-perspective or Creative Systems Theory's larger picture of human possibility.[7]

Rewriting History

Oscar Wilde wrote, "The one duty we owe to history is to rewrite it." The application of a creative frame goes a long way toward doing so. Traditional notions tend to reduce history to a chronicling of leaders, wars, and technologies. And more recent "big history" efforts rarely get us much further. The picture provided by a creative frame at the least has as much to do with ourselves as what we might invent. And ultimately it has to do with something more fundamental—human meaning and its story over time. It is important to appreciate how much we can gain from bringing evolutionary perspective of the sort we have reflected on in this chapter to history.

That contribution has multiple layers. Most immediately Creative Systems Theory Patterning in Time concepts help us see history more accurately. Certainly this is the case where traditionally we have denigrated the realities of earlier times. A creative frame helps us recognize how developmental amnesias in combination with mythologized projection have often had us confuse earlier realities with projected unsavory parts of ourselves. Patterning in Time observations provide an appreciation for what makes the realities of different times in humanity's story powerful and unique. In the process, they provide a direct antidote to the legitimate concerns that have often in times past resulted in the dismissal of evolutionary thinking.

Patterning in Time concepts also help us see history more accurately where in the past we have romantically idealized earlier

---

7 I would include twentieth-century German evolutionary philosopher Jean Gebser on my list of thinkers whose ideas have gotten at least a toe over Cultural Maturity's threshold. Gebser's formulations emphasized the importance in our time of drawing on perspectives from multiple periods in culture. His picture of the future can fall for some of the same traps as more spiritual forms of philosophical idealism and in the end is best thought of as that, but in his basic approach, he makes a serious effort to be systemic. He is careful to distinguish what he describes as a coming "integral" stage in culture from some identification with earlier times. (Jean Gebser, *The Ever-Present Origin*, Ohio University Press, 1986.)

cultural realities. Such idealizations have taken different forms depending on the time in culture that was romanticized.[8] But whatever the particular reference, Integrative Meta-perspective helps us leave behind this more elevating sort of projective distortion. The dissolving of cultural amnesias that comes with Cultural Maturity's cognitive reordering provides a clearer, if not always so reflexively affirming, picture of the past.

Another way that Patterning in Time notions contribute is by helping bring greater depth to how we understand history. Even when projection and mythologizing has not distorted our perceptions, the sensibilities that have defined Modern Age thought have caused us to miss much that is most important. Culturally Mature perspective helps us better recognize how aspects of history that we may have given secondary importance at best—such as art, music, religion, moral belief, or the life of the body—in fact have considerable pertinence to making sense of the past. It turns out that what we have missed has often been exactly that which is most essential not to miss if we wish to make sense of values, motivations, and worldviews—particularly those of premodern peoples (including ourselves prior to the Industrial Age). With Cultural Maturity's cognitive reordering, these added ingredients stop being condiments and become explicit parts of the main meal.

Patterning in Time notions also provide a picture that makes history as much about "why" as about "what." Culturally mature developmental/evolutionary perspective helps us better put past events in context and grasp how one moment of history ties to another—insights that can radically alter how we interpret circumstances. It transforms history from a chronicling of events and beliefs to a multifaceted study of human purpose and our relationship to it. While purpose has always

---

8 Romantic idealization can make association with any cultural stage. Academics may idealize the Age of Reason (or sometimes the ancient Greeks). Adamant conservative and fundamentalist religious views can by inference idealize almost medieval sensibilities (drawing on belief from a time previous to modern secular humanism and after the rise of monotheism). And New Age ideologies, along with the beliefs of environmentalists and certain feminists, may draw on idealized references to cultural times and places where archetypally feminine sensibilities held clear influence—for example, to tribal cultures, earlier agrarian societies, and classical Eastern belief.

been a part of well-told history, when we consciously bring more of ourselves to the task of understanding, history becomes more specifically
an inquiry into who we are as storytellers and makers of meaning. Also,
by implication, history becomes as much about the possible nature of
meaning in the future as it is about the stories that have brought us to
where we are today.

There is also how Creative Systems Theory's historical vantage
helps us get beyond specific traps in our thinking. Sometimes traps
are tied to sweeping pictures of history's significance. We see this with
conventional onward-and-upward interpretations. And we see it too
with contemporary views that can essentially turn traditional interpretation on its head.[9] We find an example in modern critiques of
"patriarchy" that in effect make the whole of the human story a mis-
take.[10] Today we also find traps associated with more local historical
references. With our times' increasing social and political polarization
we commonly encounter two opposite kinds of self-affirming historical distortions. We find people who patriotically glorify their country's
history and choose to ignore past blindnesses and transgressions. And
at the same time, we find others who focus only on the blindnesses
and violations and dismiss historical contributions (with commonly a
judging of the past in terms of the values and beliefs of the present).

---

9 Consistent with the concept of Reengagement, the best of historical thinking today is beginning to better appreciate the realities of times well past.
   But not surprisingly with our times' social/political climate, today we are
   also beginning to see populist big-history interpretations that exalt the
   accomplishments of early peoples and reserve their critiques for modern
   beliefs and institutions. In the end, such views represent little more than
   modern day versions of familiar romantic interpretations.

10 In *On the Evolution of Intimacy*, I describe how the fact that people often
   use the word "patriarchy" to refer to wholly different phenomena can cause
   confusion. For example, sometimes the term is used to refer to who makes
   decisions, at others to the kinds of values on which we base decisions. In
   the book, I also describe how patriarchy in the values sense is a predicted
   consequence of how change in cultural systems works. This further observation does not justify such patriarchy's continuation today, but it does
   help us get beyond using the notion either to denigrate men or to dismiss
   the whole of the human endeavor.

Integrative Meta-perspective invites us to better see actions for what they are and for what they have been, including both authentic greatness and very real pain and infliction of harm.[11]

A claim that follows from Creative Systems Theory's view of cultural change might seem particularly audacious. Not only does it map history, in a big-picture sense it predicts history. If the theory had been around 5,000 years ago (which it could not have been, given that the theory requires Integrative Meta-perspective to be fully grasped) its creative framing of development would have allowed us to anticipate the general contours of the challenges we have had to confront since that time. It is this that gives the theory the ability to assist us with understanding the present and the future.

Creative Systems Theory Patterning in Time notions also suggest an important "historical" reward beyond history itself. They make the study of history a "hands-on" tool for acquiring culturally mature perspective. Just as practicing needed new capacities, appreciating the consequences of "bridging" polarities, or more deeply engaging the complexities of intelligence can bring us closer to culturally mature understanding, so too can a sufficiently deep engagement with where we have come from. Grasping history more deeply can provide a particularly powerful way to realize the more complete kind of understanding that future tasks of all sorts will increasingly require of us.

---

11 A creative frame helps us get beyond pathologizing the past, but it does not at all deny atrocities and great injustices or propose that somehow history has always happened as it should. It does suggest that putting less-than-positive events in historical perspective can alter how we see them. For example, it notes that oppression of peoples different from one's own, colonialism, and even slavery have been recurring themes through history (with regard to slavery, we find it a common part of life in ancient Greece and Egypt and pervasive across Africa well before the European slave trade). This is not at all to dismiss such actions. Creative Systems Theory makes it a moral imperative that we judge, adding only that our judgements must be made in the context of time. Obviously acts such as these have no place in modern societies. And CST harshly judges acts from any period in history that have stopped being consistent with their time. (For example, while some might debate how I reach my conclusion, I would judge slavery in the history of the United States on that basis. In Chapter Five, I will expand on my rationale for this kind of judgement.)

CHAPTER FOUR

Beyond Projection and Mythologizing— Rethinking Human Relationship and Human Identity

Some of the insights that people find most immediately provocative—and persuasive—have to do with human relationships. They concern why in times past we have understood relationships of all sorts as we have. They also concern the mechanisms of relationship, how it is that relationships, whether more personal or more collective, have worked. They confront us with the radical recognition that never in times past have we related to others as just who they are. They also highlight the important way in which Integrative Meta-perspective makes relationship in a more complete sense for the first time possible.

A further, arguably even more radical kind of insight follows from these relationship-related observations. It has to do with identity, with what it means to be an individual human being. In a similar sense, we have never related to ourselves in any complete way. Integrative Meta-perspective doesn't let us understand ourselves objectively; indeed, it specifically confronts us with the impossibility of doing so. But it does offer that we might for the first time hold identity in a way that embraces the whole of our complexity.

These insights again bring us back to this book's essential recognition that what we believe has as much to do with how we think as what we are thinking about. Creative Systems Theory highlights how relationships through history have never involved whole systems relating to whole systems. Relationship has always before depended on the twin mechanisms of projection and mythologizing. Projection involves attributing aspects of our personal and collective selves to other individuals and larger systems—giving away parts of our whole-box-of-crayons systemic complexity. Mythologizing refers to distortions—

some of which idealize, others of which denigrate—that accompany such projection. These twin mechanisms have been central to how relationships have functioned in times past and also key to how we have tolerated the implications of relationship. Similarly, they have been necessary to past concepts of identity. The addition of Creative Systems patterning concepts fills out this picture by providing insight into how both relationships and identity have manifested in different ways at different historical times and places.

Here first I'll touch briefly on three kinds of relationships, each of which I have addressed extensively through the years—those between nations and larger groups, those between leaders and followers in authority relationships, and those between partners in love relationships. I'll then turn to what all of this has to tell us about what it means to be a person, and in particular, how what it means to be a person changes in a culturally mature reality. I'll then briefly address gender—a topic that relates to both relationship and identity—and look in particular at what Creative Systems Theory can tell us about how we have thought about it in times past and what may become different in the future. And I'll conclude with some brief reflections on contemporary "identity politics" and how it presents traps for both the political right and the political left.

Some of the observations that I will make here are less radical than just part of good psychological thinking. But many reflect specifically new insights, ones that require Integrative Meta-perspective if they are to make full sense. They are radical both in what they reveal about experience and what they have to teach us about what going forward effectively as a species will require of us. Much in the changes that I will describe is beyond what we can currently easily grasp or certainly make manifest. But I will argue that these changes will be essential to a future that is healthy and vital.

Getting Beyond Our Need for "Evil Empires"

Let's start with relationships between nations and social groups. Historically, it has been rare that we have seen peoples who are different from ourselves, even those who reside at a parallel point in cultural development, at all clearly. Indeed, often we have barely seen them at all. We find evidence with earliest cultural times in how population groups frequently developed wholly different languages even when they lived in relative proximity. And commonly, when there has been acknowledgement, differences have been polarized and distorted. We've tended to divide our world into allies and enemies—"chosen people" and "evil others."

Culturally mature perspective highlights the perhaps surprising recognition that while such us-versus-them thinking can have less-than-pleasant consequences—it has been the basis of war—in the past it has also benefitted us. Us-versus-them beliefs have protected us from a major portion of life's easily overwhelming complexities and uncertainties. They've reduced a multifaceted, multihued, often contradictory world to a more manageable black and white. They have also provided a secure, unquestioned sense of collective identity. I've observed how one of the key reasons that Cultural Maturity's changes matter is that they help us get beyond chosen-people/evil-other thinking.

Our historical need for us-versus-them thinking provides a prime illustration of how our beliefs have to do not just with what we think, but how we think. It also helps us better understand the processes that produce belief. When we divide our worlds into allies and enemies, we identify with an idealized part of our whole-box-of-crayons complexity and project an unconscious negative part onto others. The absolutism we then bring to how we view both our own kind and those we denigrate follows predictably from this cognitive mechanism.

This dynamic is not just something of our distant past. When Richard Nixon was president of the U.S., he uttered these chilling words: "It may seem melodramatic to say that the United States and Russia represent Good and Evil, Light and Darkness, God and the Devil. But if we think of it that way, it helps clarify our perspective in the world struggle." It is most fortunate that we did not see the outcomes we certainly could have.

As important as understanding the past benefits of chosen-people/evil-other thinking and its mechanisms is recognizing how such thinking has ceased to be an option. With today's growing availability of weapons of mass destruction, the possibility of catastrophic outcomes has never been higher. And the fact that addressing so many of the most critical challenges ahead for us as a species—climate change, divisive economic disparities, and the risks of pandemic, to name just a few—will require global cooperation dramatically amplifies the dangers of thinking in ways that separate the world's people into opposing camps. If we are to have a world that works for anyone, it is essential that we learn to relate collectively in more mature ways.

The recognition that projection and mythologizing play a role in how we have seen those different from ourselves is not original to me. Psychologists have historically spoken of projecting one's "shadow" onto others. But this observation does present us with a key further question where Creative Systems Theory's contribution has major significance: Is it possible to have social identity without having enemies? Many people would argue that getting beyond ally-versus-enemy thinking is really not an option, that we have evolved to be warlike, and that is that. Given today's realities, if this is the case we can stop our inquiry right here—we are doomed. Creative Systems Theory argues that fortunately this is not the case. It proposes that at least the potential to take needed further steps is built into what makes us human. The theory proposes that the ability to get beyond thinking of identity in us-versus-them terms follows directly from how developmental processes work. More specifically, it follows from Cultural Maturity's notion of a now possible cognitive "growing up."

Culturally mature perspective's more whole-box-of-crayons vantage makes it possible to leave behind projective dynamics and engage relationships of all sorts from a more Whole-Person/Whole-System place. It reveals our past need for chosen-people/evil-other narratives to be something that may once have been developmentally important (and whose heroic stories we can still legitimately look back on and value) but that today, along with putting us at risk, also gets in the way of us being fully who we are. Reflexively viewing the world in ally-versus-enemy terms comes to feel like a historical artifact—and a dangerous one.

Are we seeing evidence that this might be possible? I think so. The fall of the Berlin Wall provides an iconic example. Few anticipated it, certainly the suddenness of its collapse. And while leaders have taken credit for it, I don't think political initiatives had much to do with what we witnessed. The cause was at once simpler and more profound. In effect, we got bored with what the wall represented. The absoluteness of belief and knee-jerk polar animosities needed to support it stopped being sufficiently compelling.

That said, dynamics that I've described now manifesting around the globe make the situation with regard to this critical question precarious. Today, we often see regression with regard to this essential new capacity. The key recognition is that any possibility of a peaceful world depends on the realization of more Whole-System relationships between the world's peoples. Hold onto the projections of times past, and Pogo's quip that "We have met the enemy and he is us" becomes not just the truth, but quite possibly the end of us.

The contribution of Creative Systems Theory with regard to relationships between nations and ethnic groups has several layers. Integrative Meta-perspective makes us-versus-them dynamics more understandable. Patterning in Time distinctions help us go a step further and tease apart the different ways such dynamics manifest at various stages in cultural development. And of particular importance for our time, CST clarifies how going forward may in fact be an option. Success at taking needed steps will depend on a significant realization of culturally mature capacities. But in a way otherwise hard to grasp, the picture the theory presents offers legitimate reason to hope that a more peaceful world in the future might be an option.[1]

Confronting Today's Crisis of Confidence in Leadership

The topic of leadership in another way confronts us with how what we think is a product of how we think. It also in a further way highlights how the kinds of changes in how we think that come with Integrative Meta-perspective fundamentally alter what we find to be true—and of particular importance, also the choices we make and how we act in the world.

Trust in leadership of all sorts today is less than it was at the height of anti-authoritarian rhetoric in the 1960s. We could easily assume—and people have argued—that this modern lack of confidence in leadership

---

1 Note that culturally mature perspective doesn't "side" with peace in some pacifistic sense. It emphasizes the importance of boundaries, and with this good defenses. And even if cultures that are furthest along in their development succeed in getting beyond the need for enemies, in much of the world this will not be the case. I'm not suggesting that we face a necessarily peaceful future, rather that our future can be tolerable only to the degree those capable of making mature choices provide leadership in doing so.

reflects something gone terribly wrong—broad failure on the part of leaders, a loss of moral integrity on the part of those being led, or even an impending collapse of society. Creative Systems Theory supports that there are very real reasons for concern. But it also offers an alternative, big-picture interpretation. If what it suggests is not the major factor now, it should be a major factor in the long term.

An essential aspect of Cultural Maturity's "growing up" is the way it makes possible a new maturity in how we understand, relate to, and embody authority. This includes authority of every sort, from that exercised in leading nations; to the expertise of teachers, doctors, or ministers; to the authority we apply in making the most intimate of personal life choices. CST observes that we now reside in a transitional time in the realization of needed, more mature leadership capacities. But it also affirms that while these are not easy circumstances, they suggest a picture that is ultimately encouraging. It may be less that leaders are failing us than that old ways of thinking about leadership are failing.

Formal leadership's evolution has involved not just what leadership looks like, but what makes it leadership at all. Leadership as we think of it arrived with the Modern Age emergence of individual determination as a rallying cry and with the rise of democratic principles. New leadership assumptions and approaches then directly challenged the more heredity-based and dictatorial/authoritarian leadership practices of earlier times. These changes represented important steps forward. But if CST is right, a further chapter in how we conceive of and engage leadership will be essential for times ahead. The reason is similar to what we saw with relationship between nations. The future will require leadership of a more Whole-Person/Whole-System sort.

The twin roles of projection and mythologizing again help us make sense of both what we have known and why more is needed. Mythologized projection has always before been central to the workings of leadership. We've projected our authority onto leaders. In the process, we've given them an elevated status. This is most obvious with leaders of times well past such as pharaohs and kings, who were seen, if not as gods, then certainly as god-like. But in a similar, if not quite so absolutist way, we have continued to make leaders heroic symbols in modern times. We described John Kennedy using the imagery of Camelot. We depicted Ronald Reagan as a mythic father figure. And we've symbolically elevated not just political leaders, but authorities of all sorts—religious leaders, professors, doctors, and leaders in business. The relationship of leaders and followers has been based on two-halves-make-a-whole systemic dynamics.

Projecting our power onto leaders has again served us. As with chosen-people/evil-other projections in relations between social groups, idealizing authority has protected us from life's easily overwhelming bigness. It has provided a sense of order in a world that would otherwise be too complex and deeply uncertain to tolerate. But going forward will require more than leadership as we have known it. If the concept of Cultural Maturity holds, the future depends on the possibility of leadership that better reflects the whole of who we are.

Do we currently see such Whole-Person/Whole-System changes in how we think about and embody authority? Given today's crisis of confidence in leadership, we could easily think otherwise. But in fact we witness changes consistent with the needed, more mature kind of leadership with authority relationships of many sorts. Some of the most important "bridgings" beginning to manifest in our time link the opposite halves of authority-related polarities—teacher and student, doctor and patient, minister and churchgoer, president and populace. Authority relationships of all sorts are becoming more two-way, with more listening and flexibility on the part of leaders and more engaged and empowered roles for those who draw on a leader's expertise and guidance. Again, these are changes that require Integrative Meta-perspective to fully grasp. And they are changes that require culturally mature capacities to become significantly manifest. But they could not be more important.

Leadership provides another illustration of the awkward in-between place that we so often find ourselves in today when it comes to Cultural Maturity's changes. We may want leaders to get off their pedestals, but frequently when they attempt to do so, we respect them less, not more. We want leaders to be more transparent, to reveal more of themselves, and to make fewer decisions behind closed doors; however, when they do, our first response is often to attack them for their human frailties. We tend to be much better at demanding the gift of culturally mature leadership than at knowing what to do with it. But even this is a start. And it is a start toward a kind of change that should more and more reshape how we give expression to authority.

Beyond Romeo and Juliet—and the Future of Love

That we might encounter a related evolutionary story with intimate relationships can take people by surprise. Indeed, we can find the whole notion that love changes at all surprising. We tend to think of love as timeless—love is love. But, in fact, romantic love as we think of it is a relatively recent cultural "invention"—a product of our Modern Age. (We idealized romantic love in the European Middle Ages, but it was unrequited love that we put on a pedestal, not our modern version.) And if people do recognize that changes have taken place through history, they tend to assume that love as we know it represents a kind of culmination.

But it doesn't take too close a look to realize that our modern definition too has limitations. I first wrote about how love today is changing over three decades ago in an article I titled "A New Meaning for Love." No piece I've written since has been more often cited. Changes reshaping love similarly require Integrative Meta-perspective to deeply grasp and culturally mature capacities if we are to make them fully manifest. But both Creative Systems Theory and my experience as a therapist working with couples suggest that love that can work going forward will depend on these changes. It is a topic I addressed in depth in my book *On the Evolution of Intimacy*.

It turns out that not only is the Modern Age Romeo and Juliet picture not some final ideal, it represents something quite different from what we have assumed it to be about. We tend to think of romantic love as love between individuals. Modern romantic love did take us an important step toward individual choice beyond having mates chosen by families or matchmakers. But romantic love is not about loving as individuals in the sense of loving as two whole people. Again we find bonds based on projection and mythologizing. We project parts of ourselves and mythologize the other, making that person our answer, our brave knight or fair lady, our completion (or, at less pleasant moments, the great cause of our suffering). Romantic love as we commonly think of it is two-halves-make-a-whole love.

Such two-halves-make-a-whole mechanisms again have served us. Indeed, they have been essential to love in times past being possible. Much of the "glue" of relationship, the magnetism of love and the basis of commitment, has come from this giving of dimensions of ourselves to the other for safekeeping. Love has been based on illusion, but it is illusion only in the sense that from our present perspective we can glimpse fuller options. Making the other our completion in this way has protected us from uncertainties and complexities that before would have been too much for us.

But Modern Age romantic love remains yet short of the kind of greater completeness—of both identity and love—that Cultural Maturity predicts will be needed going forward. One of the best places to see the difference between Modern Age romantic love and culturally mature, Whole-Person connecting concerns what tends to happen when a love relationship ends. When relationships based on romantic projection end, they tend not to do so pleasantly. We expect that we will dislike the other person and most often do. The reason is not hard to understand from what I have described. Separation requires that we extract the projected parts of ourselves. Commonly, we create the needed distance by replacing the idealized projections that drew us together with projections of an "evil other" sort. Whole-Person love relationships tend to end differently. There can be significant disappointment and sadness that things no longer work as they have, and deep grieving at the loss. There can also be regret that mistakes were made. But unless there has been some unforgivable violation, there tends to be gratitude for what was shared even if ultimate dreams could not be fulfilled. Often people remain friends in some way.

Today we witness the beginnings of an important "growing up" in our relationship to love. We see its beginnings in today's challenging of traditional gender roles. And now and then too we glimpse the option of loving in more complete ways. As with mature relations between nations (that leave behind our past need for "chosen people" and "evil empires") or between leaders and followers (a kind of relationship that has always before been based on a "parent and child" mythologizing of authority), this is a pursuit that is at once more humble and more rich (and profound) in its possibilities. Love increasingly invites us to better recognize how, as Lily Tomlin put it, "we are all in this alone." And, simultaneously, it reveals the possibility of deeper and more complete ways of being together. Such Whole-Person connecting is not some luxury. I think the future of intimacy depends ultimately on our ability to realize this new, fuller relationship with ourselves and with those we love.

We gain added perspective—not just on love, but on culturally mature understanding more generally—by noting what culturally mature love is not. Culturally mature love is not simply some final expression of individualism. Individualism provides needed separateness but by itself teaches us nothing about the needed new depth of connection. It is also fundamentally different from most more humanistic notions of wholeness in relationship—look closely and we see that such notions tend to be less about loving as whole people than about identification with the emotional side of experience. Neither is it about some postmodern, anything-goes moral relativism. Culturally mature love requires greater moral discernment, not less.

Cultural Maturity's changes make love more complex, but also, again, in important ways simpler. As far as complexity, Whole-Person love requires that we know both ourselves and the person we are with more deeply. As far as simplicity, we find it possible to leave much of the past drama of relationship behind us. Intimacy becomes more straightforward—about loving another person for just who they are. Whichever most stands out, the complexity or the simplicity, if the concept of Cultural Maturity is accurate, it is these changes that will allow love to remain something powerful in our lives. In the end, they offer not just new options in love, but the potential for more richly fulfilling bonds.

As yet we rarely see examples of mature love in the media. Romantic titillation and soap opera melodrama more often prevail. But these changes are very much happening. Forty years ago in my work with couples, it was rare for the kinds of questions that come with Whole-Person relating to play a major role. Now it is extremely rare if they do not. This makes working with couples today particularly enjoyable. It also supports hope that Cultural Maturity's changes are more in the cards than we might assume. These are changes whose time has come.

The Myth of the Individual

This chapter's reflections on relationship imply some dramatic conclusions, and not just about relationships. A big one has to do with how we have before thought about what it means to be an individual. It turns out that what we have seen historically has had little to do with being an individual, at least in any complete sense. Creative Systems

Theory calls this misconception the modern Myth of the Individual. The recognition that our Modern Age concept of individuality is based on an ultimately partial way of thinking about who we are provides some of the best evidence that a further chapter in culture's story is needed and possible.

The Myth of the Individual has three parts. Each in different ways adds to our systemic picture of understanding and further ties it to a needed next cultural chapter. First is the assumption that we have in fact been individuals. With the beginnings of our Modern Age, we celebrated a new freedom for the individual. I've described how a world of more authoritarian forms of leadership and where love's determinations were made by one's family or a matchmaker gave way to a reality in which we experienced choice as laying increasingly in our hands. But this realization of the individual was illusionary, or at least partial and preliminary. In each case, what we've witnessed has been based on two-halves-make-a-whole dynamics. Being half of a systemic whole is not yet about being an individual, certainly not in any complete sense.

The second part of the modern Myth of the Individual concerns the assumption that individuality as we have thought of it represents an ideal and endpoint. In fact, it represents neither. Because the kind of "individuality" that we saw with heroic leadership and romantic conceptions of love was based on distorted understanding, it can't be an ideal. And because further realities are very much possible, it can't be an endpoint. Being an individual takes on a fundamentally different meaning with Cultural Maturity's changes. Individual identity becomes about more consciously holding the whole of our human complexity.

The third part of the modern Myth of the Individual concerns a more specific way in which how we have thought about individuality ultimately falls short. Restricted to past ways of thinking, we might reasonably assume that individuality, when fully realized, would be about finally becoming wholly distinct. A capacity for greater distinction is indeed very much part of what culturally mature identity gives us. Culturally mature leadership and love each involve the ability to stand more fully separate. But this capacity for greater distinction is only half of what we find. More consciously engaging the whole of our multifaceted complexity also alters identity in the sense that it deepens our capacity for connectedness. Whole-Person/Whole-System

leadership offers the possibility of deeper and more authentic engagement between leaders and those the leader represents. And in a similar way, Whole-Person love offers the possibility of more complete and
enduring intimate bonds.

This deeper connectedness is in part a product of the fact that with
Cultural Maturity's changes we better bring the whole of ourselves to
the task of relating—and are thus capable of engaging in fuller ways.
But a further factor that follows from just what human complexity includes also plays an essential role. Integrative Meta-perspective offers
that we might draw more consciously on parts of ourselves that appreciate that to live is to be connected—to others we care about, in community, with nature, and with existence more generally. This deeper capacity for connectedness cannot happen without first recognizing our
fundamental distinctness. But this additional contribution is essential
to fully realized Whole-Person identity and relationship.

The Myth of the Individual is pertinent not just to how we think
about relationships and individual identity, but also to how we conceive of human institutions—of all sorts. Common assumptions about
government make a good point of reference. We've tended to think of
modern representative government—as with Modern Age institutions
of all sorts—as an ideal and endpoint. Part of the argument for this conclusion (if we need an argument—people at every cultural stage assume
their particular reality is complete and culminating) is that modern institutional democracy is "government by the people." By this we mean
government as an expression of individual choice. But while certainly
it is the case that Modern Age democracy involves greater choice than
the governmental forms of any earlier cultural stage, the Myth of the
Individual suggests that what we have seen thus far is individual determination only of a limited sort. We have not yet witnessed government
by the people in the mature systemic sense of whole people taking full
responsibility for their choices. This will require a further step in our
evolution as choice-making beings.

I've observed several Cultural Maturity–related changes that could
contribute to a next chapter in government. I think specifically of stepping beyond seeing nation-states (and their institutions) as mythic
parents, setting aside ally-versus-enemy thinking, confronting the
limitations of partisan polarization, and leaving behind mythologized

concepts of leadership. We can now add one more that in an important way brings all the others together. Culturally mature governance becomes more authentically government by the people, government as an expression of human identity in its fully mature manifestation.

Integrative Meta-Perspective and the "Self"

A debate from my field of psychology and psychiatry helps further fill out how Cultural Maturity's changes expand our understanding of identity. It also in another way highlights how fundamentally a culturally mature picture of identity challenges past assumptions. This particular debate came to the fore in the middle of the last century, but it had its roots much earlier—indeed, we've found it in some form since the beginnings of self-reflection. Here I refer to the battle over the nature of the "self."

In this debate's modern form, behaviorists (along with the more extreme of cognitive theorists) stand on one side; those of more humanistic or spiritual bent, and certain thinkers of a more analytic inclination, on the other. Behaviorists—at least of the more absolutist right-hand sort—tend to dismiss the whole notion of a self (they make it all behavior). Those who put greater emphasis on inner reflection tend to wax poetically about the "authentic," "true," or "original" self (which therapeutic process is supposed to be about recovering).

It turns out that neither view holds up well to scrutiny. Making us only behavior leaves out not just inner experience, but any appreciation for meaning and coherence. And making identity an opposite to conditioning, belief, and the stuff of the material world in the end dismisses much that is most important in who we are as manifest and manifesting beings. The shortcomings are not just conceptual. They become obvious with clinical work that is at all deep. The approaches applied by advocates of either of these views can be useful, but they are also each vulnerable to major traps from which there are no means of escape. The best of thinkers of all persuasions will at least hint at a more complex picture. But where approaches are at all ideological, the battle will remain.

Identity as understood from the vantage of Integrative Meta-perspective is wholly different. It is systemic—more fully embracing— and in a way that explicitly includes both more inner and more outer psychological aspects. This more complete understanding of identity again requires Cultural Maturity's cognitive reordering to fully grasp. But, arguably, a meaningful sense of who we are going forward depends on it.

The challenge this new picture makes to more right-hand formulations is most easily recognized. With Integrative Meta-perspective, the idea of a self very much makes sense—indeed, a specifically living/meaning-making sort of self. Put in the metaphor I have often drawn on here, identity becomes who we are in consciously holding the whole cognitive box of crayons. Being fully oneself involves using that complexity in the most powerful and consciously congruent ways.

But opposite, more humanistic, spiritual, and analytic views are ultimately challenged just as fundamentally. Identity from the vantage of Integrative Meta-perspective involves drawing on all of our often-contradictory ways of seeing the world (more left-hand and more right-hand equally—or, more precisely, in the particular balance our temperament reflects). Self in this more complete picture becomes explicitly different from some core self or essence, and certainly different from some original essence. Self in any sense pertinent to meaning exists in time (it is not about original purity) and space (it ties in with every part of our life experience).[2]

A couple of further distinctions are important to make if these conclusions are to be ultimately helpful. First we need to distinguish identity in a culturally mature sense from what we find with ways of thinking about identity that reflect some middle ground between the extreme views that I've highlighted. It is a kind of distinction that will make more sense after I introduce an approach in the next chapter that specifically works to support Integrative Meta-perspective. It is enough at this point to note that the term "ego" in the frequently

---

2 We can make these additional distinctions more concrete by turning to how language reflects bodily experience. When such advocates speak of some "core self," they are referring to experience's most inner aspects. But more outer dimensions of who we are are just as essential to identity in any complete sense. In Chapter Six I will touch on a key practical implication of this observation. We will examine how more inner and outer aspects of experience play the appropriately larger role in people with different personality styles. Depending on how one defines "self," one's definition implies a fundamental bias with regard to who is regarded as significant.

quite different ways it is applied in psychological contexts often reflects this further kind of result.

The second distinction concerns the different ways that the self question applies to personal maturity and Cultural Maturity. I've described how the developmental challenges that come with the second half of a person's life find resolution in a more personal kind of cognitive reordering. Most therapeutic models focus on first-half-of-life developmental tasks, but a few go further to address second-half-of-life challenges. Successfully meeting the challenges of our later years results in greater self-understanding and a deeper sense of meaning. Such achievement can have major importance, but it is important to understand that this is not yet identity in the sense of Cultural Maturity. The person likely retains identification with the ideological assumptions of their time. Cultural Maturity takes us beyond not just limited personal beliefs, but also the limitations of more collective belief. When we embrace a more Whole-Person understanding of self at a cultural level, we step into a world in which ideology, rather than driving us, is perceived as a failing, as getting in the way of fully realizing what it means to be a person.[3] We see this second distinction in another way in how Cultural Maturity's changes can manifest at any time in one's life.

---

3 Psychology and psychiatry have taken steps toward a more systemic understanding of identity, at least with regard to its more personal development manifestation. Carl Jung's notion of self as depicted in his short book *The Undiscovered Self* (Carl Jung, *The Undiscovered Self*, Penguin Books, 1957) offers a good beginning description of a more complete picture of personal identity. Jung gave unusual attention to second-half-of-life personal development. At a cultural level, he at least recognized that we need more people capable of a more mature kind of personal identity. Early contributors to existential psychology, such as Rollo May and Viktor Frankl, similarly pointed toward the possibility of more complete ways of framing identity, at least at a personal level. I would also include psychologist Robert Kegan whose ideas drew from the developmental formulations of Jean Piaget in this regard. Each of these contributors got to a more complete picture through the same route, by putting questions of meaning (and a specifically systemic conception of meaning and its realization) central in their thinking about personal identity. Early twentieth-century German Gestalt psychology drew on new ideas about perception to arrive at a related kind of conclusion.

The Changing Face of Gender

The topic of gender brings together observations about relationship and identity. In *On the Evolution of Intimacy*, I address both how we have thought about it historically and how we might best understand changes we see today. I've noted that one thing I've found with the book is that few people today seem ready to look at gender-related issues with the complexity and nuance that culturally mature perspective suggests they require. I will briefly touch on the topic here because of the further way it highlights Creative Systems Theory's power as a tool for making sense of both beliefs through time and what the future may hold.

A first gender-related insight is radical in the same sense that we have seen with observations about relationship and identity more generally. Ideas about gender and gender differences in times past have again been products less of what is actually the case than of projection and mythologizing. The language of gender archetype that I've used in talking about the workings of polarity helps us be more specific.[4] Historically, our concepts of gender have been based on projected idealized/mythologized archetypal images and qualities. In *Creative Systems Theory*, I describe how our particular beliefs about gender differences through time have reflected the specific ways that gender archetype has manifested and been projected at various points in the evolution of culture. As with relationship and identity more generally, such dynamics have distorted perception. Put simply, throughout history, we've confused gender with gender archetype.

While today we appropriately question past polarized belief, once more we see dynamics that historically have served us. Projecting and mythologizing have again benefitted us by reducing uncertainty and complexity. Gender roles and polar perceptions of gender differences have been thought of as god-given (whatever our particular gods).

---

4 The need to emphasize the difference between gender and gender archetype here becomes particularly important. Men and women each manifest archetypally masculine and archetypally feminine qualities. And depending on their personality style, the balance in a man may be more archetypally feminine than in the average woman, and that in a woman more archetypally masculine than in the average man.

Without this absolutism of belief, it is unlikely that we could have tolerated the questions that gender identity and right behavior between the sexes present. And projecting and mythologizing, by supporting division of labor, offered that we might interact in complementary ways.

But how we think about gender today is changing, dramatically. Not only are gender roles being challenged on all fronts, we are beginning to think of gender itself more fluidly and complexly. Creative Systems Theory adds important nuance to our understanding of just what is changing. Commonly these changes are thought of only in terms of progress—as finally beginning to get things right. The theory supports much in this conclusion. But it also proposes that if we wish to fully make sense of today's changes and what might be most important in gender's future, we need to bring greater detail and sophistication to our understanding.

I find it helpful to think of what we find today in terms of three different change mechanisms. Each is familiar from our previous look at the evolution of narrative. Some of what we witness can best be thought of as a culminating expression of Modern Age developmental dynamics, the kind that gave us the Bill of Rights and all the equality-related efforts that have followed in centuries since. The contribution with this first kind of mechanism is today's greater appreciation for equal rights and equal opportunity.

We also see changes that are products of more postmodern (Transitional) mechanisms. Here the emphasis is on setting aside past cultural expectations and constraining beliefs. The contribution of this second dynamic is a world in which options become in principle infinite and ultimately ours to determine. That includes not just how we choose to behave, but how we conceive of what it means to be gendered.

But we also see changes that begin to reflect Cultural Maturity–related mechanisms. We may not be so conscious of just what is going on, but the results, at least in the long term, should be even more consequential. We are starting to leave behind the projections and mythologizings that in times past have been key to our understandings of gender. With Integrative Meta-perspective, we better recognize how men and women each embody both archetypally masculine and archetypally feminine characteristics.(Note that one implication of this insight is that psychologically we all become in an important sense "non-binary.") We also see how an appreciation of this fact makes for more complete understandings of identity and also the possibility of more fulfilling bonds, whether between men and women or in same-sex relationships. Identity and relationship become defined increasingly in Whole-Person terms.

What Cultural Maturity adds to the gender conversation will be new to many people, but what I just described is unlikely to provoke great controversy. It simply helps fill out what changes we see involve. But there are also conclusions that follow from Cultural Maturity's changes where that is not the case. Here, I will touch on just one that is particularly pertinent to the topic of identity. It has to do with a key difference between where Modern Age changes and Cultural Maturity's further cognitive reordering take us. Modern Age advocacy tends to make the ultimate task equality and stop there. In contrast, culturally mature perspective is careful not to confuse equality with equivalence.

With regard specifically to gender, in adding the essential recognition that men and women each embody archetypally masculine and feminine characteristics, Cultural Maturity's more systemic picture further affirms that men and women are more similar than we have tended to assume in times past. But it also helps us better appreciate normative differences. Today, the suggestion that we might find differences of any kind between men and women can be controversial. Contemporary academic thought may claim that psychological differences, if they exist at all, are products only of conditioning, of the different ways that boys and girls are raised. Indeed, it is possible in academia today to lose one's job simply for suggesting the existence of differences of a more fundamental sort. But the fact of real differences seems obvious to most people. Very few individuals who spend much time around young children, for example, would find the conclusion that all we need is upbringing to explain apparent differences at all persuasive.

How are men and women in fact different—if they are at all? At the least we live in different kinds of bodies. Given how both Modern Age thought and the different-strokes-for-different-folks assumptions of postmodern belief each point toward what is, in effect, a disembodied future, the fact that we have different kinds of bodies might seem of minor significance. But this can't ultimately be our direction going forward. A key characteristic of Cultural Maturity's changes, one we will examine more closely in the next chapter, is that they help us get more in touch with the body as experience.

We gain important further insight by turning to observations about the relative balance of psychological characteristics. While here necessarily we are dealing with generalities, they prove useful. Once we leave behind polarized expectations, along with finding greater individual variation, we also better recognize normative differences. Men on average tend to embody a bit more of the archetypally masculine; women tend on average to embody somewhat more of the archetypally feminine. I think of about a 60/40 balance of archetypal qualities relative to gender.[5]

Such recognition of normative differences requires that we think in ways that we may not be used to, but it can be powerfully freeing. Simultaneously, it takes us beyond history's polarized expectations and unisex notions that in their own ways can be just as constraining. Suddenly our gender options multiply. And our task in relationship to gender becomes newly clear and obvious: to simply be as fully ourselves as we are able.[6]

---

5 Body dynamics support this conclusion. Note that men tend to carry their center of balance somewhat higher in the body, in the chest and shoulders, and women somewhat lower, in the pelvis and thighs. And even with the same amount of exertion and conditioning, men's bodies tend to be a bit harder to the touch and women's a bit softer. A person could dismiss these observations as "just physical." But, again, as CST makes clear, the notion that anything is just physical is more a product of our time in culture than how things actually work. Reflection on personality style differences in Chapter Six will expand on this kind of observation.

6 Some of the writers who are most often cited by students of women's issues make reference to related kinds of difference. For example, in her powerfully influential book *In a Different Voice*, psychologist Carol Gilligan, drawing on her studies of moral development in children, spoke of male experience in terms of "a self defined more through separation" and female experience in terms of "a self defined more by connection" (p.35, Harvard University Press, 1982). Linguist Deborah Tannen reached similar conclusions in her bestselling book *You Just Don't Understand: Women and Men in Conversation* (Ballantine, 1990) in contrasting how women are more apt to use communication to establish social bonds and men are more apt to use communication to solve problems.

This more systemic way of thinking about gender differences will for many people lessen the controversy, but given that much of conflict in belief tends to be a product of ideology, we should not expect it to get rid of controversy entirely. And implications with regard to more specific gender-related questions can arouse intense feelings even among those who might not have any difficulty with the basic picture that I've described.

Current debates about equality in the workplace provide a good example. Equal opportunity and equal pay for equal work are unquestionable goods. But we can hear it implied that if we find gender differences in the number of people in particular professions, the only legitimate explanation is discrimination. Very often, discrimination is the major factor. But the recognition that we see normative differences also suggests other possibilities. What we are most attracted to, for example, could also play a role. Some jobs are going be more appealing to those with more of the archetypally masculine in their makeup, others to those who most manifest the archetypally feminine. That will be the case for both men and women, but if the idea of a 60/40 normative balance is accurate, there are going to be normative differences too in the jobs men and women are drawn to. Fifty years from now, differences should be less extreme than what we see today, and certainly much less extreme than we have seen historically. But even if discrimination with regard to job opportunity is totally eliminated, in most professions discrepancies will likely remain. I suspect we will still see more male firefighters and racecar drivers. And nurses and teachers of young children will likely still more often be women.

This kind of observation has implications beyond just job preference. It extends to how a person's balance of more archetypally masculine and archetypally feminine characteristics may influence more general life choices. A surprising outcome we find in Nordic countries (where gender equality is highest and best supported by social policy) is provocative in this regard. Rather than more women senior business managers as we might expect, in fact we are finding fewer.[7] Framing

---

7 The percentage of senior business managers in Nordic countries who are women is 31% compared to 43% in the United States, for example. See Nima Sanandaji, *The Nordic Gender Equality Paradox*, Timbro, Stockholm, 2016.

these results in terms of gender archetype helps get us beyond thinking only in terms of men and women. It may be that when people for whom the archetypally feminine plays a strong role in their makeup are given more choices, many will find the rat race not where they want to spend their years.

I've described how culturally mature perspective confronts ideological correctnesses of both the political left and the political right. These reflections on gender, the workplace, and more general life choices provide good examples. Those on the Left are likely to bristle at any suggestion that differences are not simply a product of discrimination. Those on the Right are more likely to feel there is something sacred in traditional roles. Framing what we see in terms of gender archetype and the evolution of culture offers the possibility of thinking in more nuanced ways. Chapter Six looks briefly at the Creative Systems Personality Typology. The picture the typology presents further fills out these observations by helping us better think in terms of individual variation. It describes how personality style differences reflect different balances and relationships of archetypal qualities.[8]

How Identity Politics Stops Us in Our Tracks

A chapter in my book *Perspective and Guidance for a Time of Deep Discord* addresses an important further identity-related issue—how social and political discourse today so often gets described in the language of "identity politics." It is important to recognize that identity as used in the phrase "identity politics" stops well short of the complete sort that comes with Integrative Meta-perspective. This could seem to be only an issue of semantics, but one consequence of this difference is that while contemporary identity politics tends to be thought of in terms of progress, advancement is often less the result than advocates like to assume.

---

8 In Chapter Three, I described how CST's particular evolutionary approach helps us get beyond judging past events according to the values of the present. Gender-related observations such as these provide further illustration. This kind of perspective can be extended to larger cultural contexts. We find a good example in how people in the West can assume that the wearing of the hijab or burka in the Middle East reflects only gender oppression. When understood in the context of Middle-Axis dynamics in the evolution of culture, we see a picture that is significantly more complex.

An increasingly prevalent and dangerous consequence of identity politics helps clarify why this is what we would predict. Identity politics tends to define identity in victim terms. Too often, we find ourselves in a reality of competing victim narratives in which we somehow assume that the person or group that can feel most mistreated and misjudged wins. In the end, it is a competition in which nobody wins. Victim narratives distort our thinking and make it impossible for anyone to effectively move forward. In the end, they reflect but the other side of the coin to the dominance narratives of times past.

Victim narratives increasingly define identity on both the political right and the political left. This is particularly the case at ideology's populist extremes. From the populist Right we hear victim narratives described in response to college-educated coastal elites, critical race theory, and government encroachment on individual freedoms with vaccine mandates. From the populist Left we hear them framed in the language of patriarchy, racism of an all-encompassing systemic sort, gender discrimination, and white privilege.

Perceived historical injustices and inequalities are often very real—and not infrequently horrendously so. As I touched on in the previous chapter, we gain much by seeing history clearly, including its very significant warts and often glaring time-specific transgressions. The ability to do so reflects an important kind of advancement in our time.

But defining oneself as a victim is different. When we can get no further than the language of trauma and victimization, not only do we end up again thinking simplistically about complex dynamics, we end up responding in ways that quite specifically get in the way of moving forward.

Psychologically, victim narratives—and particularly today's idealization of the angry victim—are in the end little different from the stories we've told in times past to justify bigotry and war. We make another the symbolic cause of all our pain. We focus on grievances and attribute what we feel in response to some "evil other." The price we pay goes well beyond just simple-minded conclusions and historical distortions. We make conversation of a culturally mature sort essentially impossible.

Most immediately, because victim narratives create worlds of us versus them, instead of supporting mutual understanding, they produce thinking that sets us even further apart. As any good psychologist knows, people who see the world in victim terms tend to be some of the quickest to victimize. At the least they are just as vulnerable as an oppressor of failing to find humanity in the other. Growing even further apart is what we have seen over recent decades wherever identity politics has come to define debate.

Of even greater importance if one's concern is real change, victim narratives are ultimately disempowering—and in a particularly insidious way. When we place all responsibility outside ourselves, we also, in the end, put authority outside ourselves. We blind ourselves not just to the complexity of perspective needed to effectively make change, but also the necessary agency and initiative—in general, and also in relation to exactly the kind of change that we might most hope to foster.

The assumptions of identity politics almost always capture important aspects of larger truths. And sometimes such advocacy can provide limited benefit, at least in the short term. But identity politics tends ultimately to be more about feeling secure in one's ideological superiority and cementing bonds of allegiance than the maturity of perspective on which essential change depends. Even when it has its roots in legitimate observations and commendable impulses, identity defined in this way tends to get in the way of where we need to go. We need to do better if our efforts are to be ultimately effective.

CHAPTER FIVE

Truth, Intelligence, Meaning, and How Our Thinking Can Go Astray

Cultural Maturity's cognitive reordering fundamentally alters our relationship with truth. We've made a start as far as what it helps us step beyond. I've described how it challenges the unquestioned shared truths that come with a parentally conceived relationship with culture. And I've observed how it similarly takes us past the various ideology-based ways of thinking found at particular times in culture. We've also seen how the postmodern conclusion that truth is ultimately ours to determine can get us only part of the way.

We are left with the questions of just what truth then becomes. Here, too, we've made a beginning. I've described how Cultural Maturity's needed "growing up" produces truth that is more complete (and ultimately "common sense") than either utopian or dystopian beliefs. I've observed how Integrative Meta-perspective replaces the heroic and romantic narratives of times past with a more systemic picture of what creates significance. We've looked at how a creative frame offers a new foundation for understanding truth, a new kind of Fundamental Organizing Concept, and we've begun to apply this insight with Patterning in Time notions that bring detail to how truths in systems of all sorts evolve. And I've touched on how truth's evolving picture manifests in how we experience relationships of all sorts—and ultimately in how we understand what it means to be a person.

All of these observations have been radical in that they point toward something fundamentally new. And the concepts they highlight have each been radical for the same basic reason. Each is systemic in a sense that becomes fully graspable only with Integrative Meta-perspective. This chapter addresses a handful of further truth-related insights from Creative Systems Theory. Each again follows from the specific kind of systemic vantage that becomes possible when we have at least a toe into culturally mature territory.

We'll begin with a closer look at the critical recognition that intelligence is plural. I've described how intelligence's multiplicity is key to our striking toolmaking capacities. It also underlies how we understand truth—of all sorts. Then we will turn to Creative Systems Theory's most basic truth-related notions, what it calls Whole-Person/Whole-System patterning concepts, and examine two of particular importance. Next, I'll touch briefly on the methodology that most reliably produces culturally mature truth. We will then examine common truth-related traps and how we can understand them in terms of polarity and its creative underpinnings. And I'll conclude with reflections on how today's increasing social and political polarization—and Transitional Absurdities more broadly—threaten to distance us irretrievably from the more complete kinds of truth that will be necessary for a healthy, and perhaps even just survivable, future.

Intelligence's Creative Multiplicity

No topic more directly relates to the topic of truth than intelligence. I've emphasized how what we perceive to be true is always as much a function of how we understand as what there may be to understand. Intelligence is what we understand with. With Cultural Maturity's cognitive reordering, the truth-related recognition that intelligence is multiple comes to have special importance. We've seen how Integrative Meta-perspective involves at once more fully stepping back from and more deeply engaging the whole of our cognitive complexity. Intelligence's multiple aspects provide one of the best ways to think about that complexity.

The fact that intelligence has multiple aspects has been framed in different ways through the last century, but Creative Systems Theory's framing of intelligence's multiplicity brings particular depth and nuance to understanding.[1] The theory clarifies how, along with our ra-

---

1   The most commonly cited description of multiple intelligences today is Howard Gardner's seven-part framework. While it lacks the depth and conceptual associations of Creative Systems Theory's approach, people in education in particular find it of significant value. (Howard Gardner, *Frames of Mind*, Basic Books, 2011).

tionality, intelligence includes more emotional, imaginal, and bodily aspects. And it describes how these various intelligences work together to make us the toolmaking, meaning-making—we could say simply creative—beings that we are.

Attempting to make sense of intelligence's multiple aspects played a key early role in my thinking. At that time, intelligence's multiplicity was only beginning to be acknowledged. With my inquiries into creative process, it became clear to me that creative dynamics drew on a variety of different ways of knowing and did so in specific ways at different points along the way. It also became clear that I would need to give some special attention to intelligence's more creatively germinal sensibilities—its kinesthetic/body aspects and also its more imagination/symbol-making dimensions. At our time in culture, these ingredients in intelligence's workings tend to be particularly foreign to us. If people are conscious of such sensibilities at all, they tend not to think of them as intelligence. Work I did with Joseph Campbell, one of our time's most respected chroniclers of myth and symbol,[2] and Stanley Keleman, an early innovator in body-related psychotherapeutic approaches,[3] helped fill out my understanding of the role of intelligence's more germinal aspects in creativity's workings.

Over time, I came to recognize that the fact that intelligence had multiple aspects had much broader implications. As I was introduced in my training to developmental psychology—and in particular, more systemic developmental thinkers such as Jean Piaget[4] and Lawrence Kohlberg[5]—I was struck by how an acknowledgement of intelligence's multiple aspects was needed to at all deeply understand individual development. I also saw that essential parallels existed with what I had observed for creative dynamics.

Eventually I came to appreciate the importance of engaging intelligence's multiplicity in all parts of our lives. In particular I saw its

---

2 Joseph Campbell, *The Power of Myth*, Anchor Books, 1991.

3 Stanley Keleman, *Your Body Speaks Its Mind*, Center Press, 1975.

4 Jean Piaget, *The Language and Thought of the Child*, Routledge, 2001.

5 Lawrence Kohlberg, *The Psychology of Moral Development*, Harper and Row, 1984.

critical relationship to the tasks of Cultural Maturity. I've described how culturally mature understanding requires that we consciously draw on the whole of ourselves as cognitive systems. Integrative Meta-perspective "bridges" facts with feelings, the workings of the imagination with more practical considerations, and observations of the mind with things only our bodies can know. I came to see how understanding any culturally mature concept at all fully demands drawing in an integrated way on the full complexity of intelligence's workings.

The role of intelligence's multiplicity with personal maturity helps highlight the critical significance of the cultural implications. We associate the best of thinking in our later years not just with knowledge, but with wisdom. Knowledge can be articulated quite well by the intellect alone, but wisdom requires a more fully embodied kind of intelligence, one that draws on all of who we are. We see it not just because we better include all the aspects of our questions, but also because, when seeking answers, we don't leave out essential parts of ourselves. If the concept of Cultural Maturity is correct, we should expect an analogous result at a species level. And it is essential that we do. The future will require something beyond just being smarter in the decisions we make. Given the magnitude of the choices we confront and the potential consequences if we choose poorly, it is essential that our decisions be not just intelligent, but wise.

A Creative Framing of Multiple Intelligences

Our toolmaking nature means that human intelligence must at least powerfully support formative process. I've briefly introduced Creative Systems Theory's argument that human intelligence is specifically structured to do so. The theory proposes that we are the uniquely creative creatures we are not just because we are conscious, but because of the ways that the various aspects of our intelligence work, and in particular, how they work together.

Creative Systems Theory describes how our various intelligences—or we might better say "sensibilities," to reflect all that they encompass—relate in specifically creative ways. And it delineates how different ways of knowing, and different relationships between ways of knowing, predominate at specific times in any human change processes. The way CST ties the underlying structures of intelligence to patterns we see in how human systems change both helps us better understand change and hints at the possibility of better predicting change.

Creative Systems Theory delineates four basic types of intelligence. For ease of conversation, I will refer to them here simply as the intelligences of the body, the imagination, the emotions, and the intellect. (The theory uses the fancier language that I include in Figure 5-1.) CST proposes that these different ways of knowing represent not just diverse approaches to processing information, but the windows through which we make sense of our worlds—and more than this, the formative tendencies that lead us to shape our worlds in the ways that we do.

The theory also argues that our various intelligences work together in ways that are not just collaborative, but specifically creative. It describes how human intelligence is uniquely configured to support creative change—to drive and facilitate its workings. Our various modes of intelligence, juxtaposed like colors on a color wheel, function together as creativity's mechanism. That wheel, like the wheel of a car or a Ferris wheel, is continually turning, continually in motion. The way the various facets of intelligence juxtapose makes change, and specifically purposeful change, inherent to our natures. The following diagram depicts these associations between the workings of intelligence and the stages of formative process:

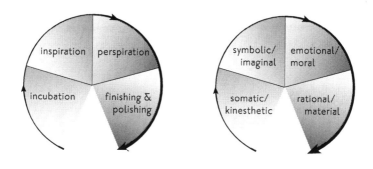

The Stages of Formative Process   Multiple Intelligences

Fig. 5-1. Formative Process and Intelligence

In Chapter Three I outlined how Creative Systems Theory maps the workings of formative process, putting greatest emphasis on the creative interplay of polar relationships. There I hinted at intelligence's role in what I described, but the topic of how intelligence manifests in evolving ways with each creative stage is sufficiently pivotal that it deserves separate treatment. Here I'll briefly describe that progression starting with a simple creative act.

With creativity's Pre-Axis, "incubation" stage, the dominant intelligence is the kinesthetic, body intelligence if you will. It is like I am pregnant, but don't yet know with quite what. What I do know takes the form of "inklings" and faint "glimmerings," inner sensings. If I want to feed this part of the creative process, I do things that help me to be reflective and to connect in my body. I take a long walk in the woods, draw a warm bath, build a fire in the fireplace.

With creativity's Early-Axis, "inspiration" stage, the dominant intelligence is the imaginal—that which most defines art, myth, and the let's-pretend world of young children. The products of this period in the creative process may appear suddenly—Archimedes's "eureka"—or they may come more subtly and gradually. It is this stage, and this part of our larger sensibility, that we tend to most traditionally associate with things creative.

With creativity's Middle-Axis, "perspiration" stage, the dominant intelligence is different still, more emotional and visceral—the intelligence of heart and guts. It is here that we confront the hard work of finding the right approach and the most satisfying means of expression. We also confront limits to our skills and are challenged to push beyond them. The perspiration stage tends to bring a new moral commitment and emotional edginess. We must compassionately but unswervingly confront what we have created if it is to stand the test of time.

With creativity's Late-Axis, "finishing and polishing" stage, rational intelligence comes to have the more dominant role. This period is more conscious and more concerned with aesthetic precision than the periods previous. It is also more concerned with audience and outcome. It brings final focus to the creative work, offers the clarity of thought and nuances of style needed for effective communication.

I've described how the cognitive changes that come with the second half of any formative process produce a more integrative picture. With creative process's second half, we step back from the work and appreciate it with new perspective. We become more able to appreciate the relationship of the work to its creative contexts, both to ourselves and to the time and place in which it was created. Specifically with regard to intelligence, we come to use our diverse ways of knowing more consciously together. We become better able to apply our intelligences in various combinations and balances as time and situation warrant, and through this to engage the work as a whole and ourselves as a whole in relationship to it.

We can again tie this progression to formative processes of all sorts. We see something similar whether our concern is an act of innovation, personal psychological development, or culture and its evolution. For example, we find the same bodily intelligence that orders creative "incubation" playing a particularly prominent role in the infant's rhythmic world of movement, touch, and taste. The realities of early tribal cultures also draw deeply on body sensibilities. Truth in tribal societies is synonymous with the rhythms of nature and, through dance, song, story, and drumbeat, with the body of the tribe.

And we find the same imaginal intelligence that we saw ordering creative "inspiration" taking prominence in the play-centered world of the young child. We also hear it voiced with particular strength in early civilizations—such as in ancient Greece or Egypt, with the Incas and Aztecs in the Americas, or in the classical East—with their mythic pantheons and great symbolic tales.

We find the same emotional and moral intelligence that orders creative "perspiration" occupying center stage in adolescence with its deepening passions and pivotal struggles for identity. It can also be felt with particular strength in the beliefs and values of the European Middle Ages, times marked by feudal struggle and ardent moral conviction (and, today, in places where struggle and conflict seem to be forever recurring).

And in a similar way, we find the same rational intelligence that comes forward for the "finishing and polishing" tasks of creativity taking new prominence in young adulthood, as we strive to create our unique place in the world of adult expectations. This more refined and refining aspect of intelligence stepped to the fore culturally with the Renaissance and the Age of Reason and, in the West, has held sway into modern times.

Finally, and of particular pertinence to the concept of Cultural Maturity, we find the same more consciously integrative relationship to

intelligence that we see in the "seasoning" stage of a creative act ordering the unique developmental capacities—the wisdom—of a lifetime's
second half. We can also see this same more integrative relationship
with intelligence just beneath the surface in our current cultural stage
in the West in the advances that have transformed understanding
through the last century.

We associate the Age of Reason with Descartes's assertion that "I
think, therefore I am." We could make a parallel assertion for each of
these other cultural stages: "I am embodied, therefore I am"; "I imagine, therefore I am"; "I am a moral being, therefore I am"; and, if the
concept of Cultural Maturity is accurate, "I understand maturely and
systemically—with the whole of myself—therefore I am." The concept
of Cultural Maturity proposes that the words you have just read about
intelligence's creative workings have made sense because such consciously integrative dynamics are beginning to reorder how we think
and perceive.[6]

Applying Intelligence's Multiplicity

Creative Systems Theory proposes that understanding most anything about us with real depth requires drawing on all of intelligence's
multiple aspects. And it describes how doing so in newly conscious and
complete ways is central to the kind of understanding our future will
increasingly require. This is the case whether the needed understanding is more personal or deals with life's most ultimate concerns.

---

6 We can think of modern psychiatry and psychology in terms of a new,
   more conscious recognition of the importance of intelligence's multiplicity.
   Freud's notion of the unconscious at least acknowledged the significance
   of aspects of ourselves beyond the rational. And key figures who followed
   brought attention to how unconscious forces could be understood not just
   in terms of repressed impulses, but also as expressions of generative dynamics that drew on nonrational aspects of intelligence. Wilhelm Reich highlighted body aspects of intelligence, Carl Jung the imaginal and mythic,
   and more humanistic voices in the later half of the last century such as Carl
   Rogers more feeling/emotional sensibilities. Near the end of the century we
   saw rationality-based approaches such as Aaron Beck's cognitive behavioral methods given greatest emphasis, in part because they are simpler to
   use, but I suspect also because they better conform to a rational/material
   worldview.

One example is particularly pertinent to Cultural Maturity's task. I've described how Transitional dynamics can leave people wandering aimlessly with no real sense of direction in their lives—what I have referred to as our time's Crisis of Purpose. And I've proposed that the way Cultural Maturity's changes help us more deeply address meaning in our lives provides an antidote. Just how this works relates directly to the way Integrative Meta-perspective better taps the full complexity of intelligence's workings. Engaging emotional intelligence along with the rational helps us get beyond the looking-out-for-number-one assumptions of mass material culture and more deeply appreciate the role of relationships in our lives. Engaging imaginal intelligence—with its language of image, myth, and metaphor—helps us more directly experience existence as something that inspires. And engaging body intelligence helps us experience more fully from the deepest layers of our living natures.

The concept of Cultural Maturity really makes sense only if we appreciate the role of intelligence's multiplicity. We can think of more consciously and fully tapping intelligence's multiple aspects as what culturally mature understanding is most ultimately about. And if we examine the skills and capacities that I've described becoming newly possible with Cultural Maturity's changes, we find that none of them can be understood with the intellect alone. Each requires all the crayons in intelligence's systemic box either to make real sense or to be effectively made manifest.

The same is the case for Creative Systems Theory more generally. In contrast to most conceptual approaches, fully grasping any CST concept requires drawing on all of intelligence's multiple aspects. We've just seen how this is true for the theory's Patterning in Time distinctions. But it is just as much the case with more here-and-now, Patterning in Space systemic concepts such as with the Creative Systems Personality Typology. The typology describes how individuals who choose to become artists, actors, teachers, engineers, scientists, or stockbrokers are different not just because their interests differ, but also because their cognitive structures reflect different preferences and balances within intelligence's multiplicity.

Contemporary thinking even at its best most often stops well short of fully grasping the depths of intelligence's workings. I've suggested that modern academic thought tends to be less helpful than we might hope when it comes to addressing essential challenges of our time. A simple explanation is that only rarely does it get beyond the equating of intelligence with rationality. I've noted how we see beginning attempts in academia to think more systemically about human understanding with what is commonly called "cognitive science." But such efforts to this point only serve to highlight how fundamentally our thinking is limited when we fail to grasp all that intelligence involves. For example, a popular cognitive science proponent not too long ago concluded that music is best thought of as "auditory cheesecake," a secondary phenomenon with no real evolutionary significance. It is hard to imagine someone who had actually been touched by music reaching this conclusion.[7] Up until recently we encountered a related kind of limited understanding with how dreams were being thought of as little more than random neural stimulation. Today, fresh attention is being given to sleep and its importance—for the establishment of long-term memory, for integration of experience, and for health more generally—but cognitive science remains a long way from fully appreciating the generative significance of what goes on during sleep.[8] Because to this point cognitive science has failed to fully recognize intelligence's deep, and deeply generative multiplicity, it has been able to address only the most surface layers of the human experience. Arguably the same is the case for the academic enterprise as a whole.

---

7   A presentation that I've often done in trainings that I call "An Evolutionary History of Music" provides a radical contrast. It uses music and dance over the course of history as a way to help people directly engage the realities of earlier periods in culture. People find it moving and powerfully effective. (See www.Evolmusic.org.)

8   Its limited view of sleep and dreaming discounts much that has been important in psychiatry's historical contribution. It also ignores experiences that people find obvious from daily experience, certainly people of more creative bent. For example, over the course of my life's work many of the most important insights have come unbidden during sleep. This happens so frequently that I sometimes find it irritating to have to awaken to write ideas down. I can't tell how much of this generation of new ideas happens during dreaming or more generally as part of the sleep process, but I would never go to sleep without paper and pen beside me.

The new picture that results when we more consciously engage the whole of intelligence's multiplicity has essential implications for this chapter's topic—just what truth becomes in a culturally mature reality. We see that only by drawing on intelligence's various aspects can we fully grasp what truth in any complete sense becomes. We also better recognize why we might expect truth to be contextually nuanced and multifaceted. And there is a further result that comes to have special importance with the application of a creative frame. As I've just implied in mapping intelligence's role in creative change, with Integrative Meta-perspective, truth in a new sense is put in motion. It becomes "exploratory." And of particular significance for a world without traditional guideposts, truth's explorations become purposeful. In the end they become about whatever thoughts and actions at a particular time and place serve to make us more. Creative Systems Theory helps us appreciate guiding principles and patterns in this newly exploratory, purpose-centered sort of truth.[9]

Human Intelligence and Artificial Intelligence

We can also apply an appreciation of intelligence's creative multiplicity to specific cultural issues. Earlier, I promised to return to one that

---

9 Psychologist Abraham Maslow, another person I would include on my list of people whose thinking at least begins to engage Cultural Maturity's threshold, made important early contributions to a more exploratory understanding of truth. With his emphasis on "self-actualization," he helped introduce the idea that psychology should step beyond relying wholly on pathology models and think more in terms of growth and possibility. Importantly, as far as the topic of intelligence's multiplicity, he did not just replace content with process in his thinking. He was outspoken in not falling for the growth center assumptions of his time. I take issue with certain aspects of his work. For example, with regard to the hierarchy of needs for which he is best known, I don't see needs always manifesting in the order he suggests. (I know many creative and socially committed people who are willing to sacrifice basic needs to do their good work.) And I view his emphasis on "peak experiences" putting undue focus on a limited and commonly misinterpreted aspect of growth. In addition, his reference to "self" in the phrase "self-actualization" often comes dangerously close to the self-as-essence sort of trap I made reference to in Chapter Four. But the attention he gave to the generative aspects of change rightly had major impact in his time. (See Abraham Maslow, *The Further Reaches of Human Nature*, Viking, 1971.)

warrants some focused reflection. It concerns what people commonly refer to as "artificial intelligence." Because of fundamental differences between it and human intelligence, I prefer instead to call it "machine intelligence" or "machine learning." Today, machine intelligence often provides great benefit and should continue to do so in the future. But a growing number of prominent figures have warned of potentially dire consequences. It is possible that one of the most intriguing areas of innovation in our time could prove to be our undoing. The essential insight if this is not to be the case relates to those basic differences between machine intelligence and human intelligence.

Three scenarios in which machine learning could have cataclysmic consequences are most often cited. We have already confronted the first two at a limited scale. With the first, some bad actor on the world stage wages a machine learning–based attack on a perceived enemy. The goal could be the destruction of physical infrastructure such as electrical grids and water supplies, disruption of communications networks, or as we have seen attempted in very rudimentary form with Russian interference in elections, the undermining of social and governmental structures.

The second scenario is less obvious in its destructiveness, but it is where currently we see the greatest harm. Increasingly today, our electronic devices are designed to capture our attention, pretty much whatever it takes to do so. And machine learning plays a major role in how they accomplish this. As a psychiatrist, I consider device addiction to be one of today's most pressing concerns. I've written about how its mechanisms are essentially the same as those that produce the attraction of addicting drugs. Our devices create artificial stimulation that substitutes for the bodily feedback that would normally tell us that something matters. Today, machine learning algorithms compound those mechanisms many times over, supporting the creation of what are, in effect, ever more powerful digital designer drugs. Machine learning's role in producing a world in which distraction and addiction more and more replace meaningful human activity could very well be the way it contributes most directly to our destruction.

The third kind of scenario is what people in the tech world most often point toward when they warn that machine learning could be the end of us. Systems that apply machine learning could very well come to out-compete us. It is easy to make the goal of a machine learning algorithm simply to have the algorithm propagate itself. Such algorithms can be single-minded in their competitiveness in ways that we humans will never be, and would never want to be. (In spite of how we tend to think of ourselves as competitive in a Darwinian fight-for-survival sense, thankfully we are more complex than just this.) The fact that learning with such systems can take place autonomously and is often beyond our ability to either understand or control means that we face the real risk of runaway mechanisms that could do major harm to humanity not through intent, but as an unintended consequence.

These are scary possibilities. And in their beginning manifestations, they are realities we already live with. It could easily seem that there is nothing we can do. If the machines want to take over, eventually they will. This is the conclusion that many people in the tech world aware enough to be concerned seem to be reaching. But while this could very well be our fate, I don't think it needs to be. The missing piece is the simple recognition that machine learning and human intelligence have very different mechanisms. In fact, they aren't that related at all. Machine learning largely mimics but one part of intelligence—our rationality—and it does that in only limited ways. Our rationality functions much more complexly than we tend to assume.

An essential insight that follows from those differences is critical to how human intelligence can serve as a buffer to potential dangers. While machine learning is single-minded in pursuing its goal, human intelligence is inherently more nuanced—and creative—in its workings. I've emphasized the important sense in which human intelligence is by its nature purposeful. When working with someone in therapy around questions of meaning, I know that all I need do is help the person engage the whole of themselves deeply and a greater sense of meaning and more purposeful choices will be the result. With regard to more collective questions, there is a related sense in which human intelligence is not just more sophisticated in its considerations, it is inherently moral. Most often in our daily lives we act with basic kindness, and when we look at history's big picture, we find humanity bringing ever greater complexity to its moral discernments.

There is clearly something in what it means to be human that is allied not just with advantage, but with purpose and larger good. And it is embedded deeply enough that we can think of the human narrative as a whole as a story of evolving purpose and moral capacity. We are imperfect beings. But we are also in the end creatively purposeful and moral beings. In contrast, machine learning follows the goals it is programmed for. Machine learning is a tool, and one with great potential for good. But there is nothing in it that makes it inherently good.

In our time, we easily miss this critical difference. Indeed, because we so readily idealize the technological (in effect make it our god) we can get things turned around completely. Caught in techno-utopian bliss, we can make machine learning what we celebrate. We do so at our peril. Our ultimate task as toolmakers is to be sure that we use our ever more amazing tools not just intelligently, but wisely. That starts with being able to clearly distinguish ourselves and our tools. Machine learning will provide a particularly defining test of this essential ability, one on which our very survival may depend.

Whole-Person/Whole-System Patterning Concepts

Making our way in a world without clear cultural guideposts requires new kinds of truth concepts. Patterning in Time notions like those we have touched on help us deal with temporal context. What Creative Systems Theory calls Whole-Person/Whole-System patterning concepts address what truth at its most basic becomes from the vantage of Integrative Meta-perspective. They are what most immediately points our way in a culturally mature reality.

Creative Systems Theory gives greatest attention to two specific Whole-Person/Whole-System concepts. The first relates to what choices are likely to be most life-affirming, the second to how much life we can tolerate. In the book *Creative Systems Theory*, I address them in detail and also describe other more secondary Whole-Systems notions. Here I will say just enough to highlight what makes these two notions important—and radical in the sense that this book is about.

A person might assume that Whole-Person/Whole-System patterning notions are less radical than Patterning in Time and Patterning in Space ideas that tease apart multilayered and highly nuanced contextual differences. But, in fact, many people find Whole-Person/ Whole-System patterning concepts the more challenging to fully get their minds around. These concepts no less require Cultural Maturity's cognitive changes to fully grasp and to effectively put into practice. And because these concepts are more direct and spare than their more differentiated cousins, people can find them more difficult to hold with confidence.

We can think of Whole-Person/Whole-System patterning concepts in opposite ways that highlight their radical newness. Because they get directly at what gives a thought or action meaning, they are bare-boned in a way that has not before been an option. And at the same time, because they effectively include all the crayons in the systemic box, they are more complex than the truths of times past. Any apparent contradiction disappears with the recognition that both of these results follow directly from Integrative Meta-perspective's more systemic relationship to experience and understanding.

Questions of Referent and the Concept of "Aliveness:"

When making choices in a culturally mature world, we necessarily begin by asking pertinent questions of referent. We want to identify where the most purposeful possibilities lie, those that are most consistent with life. In a sense this is where we have always needed to start. But in times past, culture as parent did the larger part of the determining for us. When we step over Cultural Maturity's threshold it becomes possible to make our discernments more consciously and in a more whole-box-of-crayons manner. Creative Systems Theory speaks of seeking the appropriate more systemic or integrative referent.

CST uses the term "referent" rather than the word truth to highlight how such determinations cannot be based wholly on reason and objective determination. They require Cultural Maturity's more conscious relationships with intelligence's multiplicity. Put in generative terms, truth in this sense is what we find when we consciously honor experience's creative edge. With Integrative Meta-perspective, we engage truth in this most basic sense explicitly and with a new kind of systemic completeness.

To have simpler language, I will sometimes use the term "Aliveness" to speak of truth in this sense. The word Aliveness captures well the sense in which such truth guides us in making choices that are life-affirming. But we must take some care with this kind of shorthand. The term Aliveness refers to something wholly different than just excitement or pleasure. My early mentor Joseph Campbell is perhaps best known for stating that the truth task was to "follow one's bliss." The notion struck a ready chord in his time. But he was well aware that few things were more difficult than authentically doing so, and that the task was often hardly blissful. This distinction is fundamentally important and has become increasingly so in recent times. Much of mass culture today has become little more than a vehicle for the selling of pseudo-aliveness. We have to be ever wary of artificial substitutes for the real thing.

Discerning just where truth in this most basic sense lies necessarily challenges us deeply. Besides requiring that we draw on the whole of intelligence's multiplicity, uncertainty always plays a role, as does change and the fact of real limits. But we really don't have a choice. Given what we are needing to determine, this more spare and demanding sort of truth provides us with the most ultimately reliable guidance.

The importance of this first kind of systemic determination is most easily recognized with new questions that we face as individuals. Effective moral decision-making today requires more than just thinking through more options. We need to get more directly at what for us makes a choice moral. In a similar way, a rewarding life as a man or a woman today necessarily involves not just a willingness to question past gender dictates, but also a new and deeper relationship to ourselves as gendered beings. And thinking about identity more generally demands not just that we challenge past cultural expectation, but also that we bring a much more multifaceted picture of what creates worth to the internal conversation. In each case we are applying this first sort of Whole-System truth, basing our choices on the degree to which the result is most ultimately creative, ultimately most consistent with life.[10]

---

10 This kind of recognition has historical antecedents. The best of existentialists, from Søren Kierkegaard to Jean Paul Sartre, emphasized not just leaving behind established truths, but also engaging questions of purpose. And the pragmatism of Charles Peirce, Willam James, and John Dewey, in proposing that truth is "what works," confronted the question of what truth at its most basic becomes when we better include all that is involved. But such thinking, even at its best, represented but a first step toward the needed more fully systemic kind of truth. Engaging purpose with the required depth in the end demands Integrative Meta-perspective, something

Addressing significance in this at once more bare-boned and more encompassing manner is just as pertinent when it comes to collective challenges. The importance of rethinking the bottom-line truths of particular domains provides illustration. With any new chapter in culture's story, primary realms of activity acquire new defining truths. But the diminishing of culture's past parental influence combined with the need for more full and complex understanding means that future answers must be both more consciously arrived at and more embracing than those of times past.

The field of medicine offers a good example. Modern medicine's bottom-line measure has been to defeat death and disease—and essentially at any cost. Today this measure is incompatible not just with health care that is affordable but also with good care. Beyond Cultural Maturity's threshold, our measures need to be more systemic. They must somehow acknowledge quality of life along with the fact of life; psychological, social, and spiritual aspects of health and healing in addition to the purely physical; and not just individual health but also larger societal well-being. Health care's new yardstick must address health itself—in the fullest, most complete sense.

Similarly, education's future depends not just on rethinking educational policy, but on thinking in more encompassing ways about what education is ultimately about. We tend to take education's purpose for granted—assume it to be obvious and unchanging. But at various times in culture's story that purpose has taken very different expressions. Classroom education as we customarily think of it had its origins with the need for universal literacy if democratic governance and the Industrial Revolution were to succeed. Toward this end it has served

---

only vaguely sensed, if appreciated at all by the existentialists. And existentialists and pragmatists can be some of the first to find issues with the kind of overarching conception needed to address the question of just why different things might work best (become pragmatic) at different times and places. Creative Systems Theory helps us understand why the more personal relationship to truth that existentialism and pragmatism emphasized has today become pertinent. But it also clarifies the importance of more systemic ways of understanding what makes truth at its most basic true. And it goes on to emphasize the essential significance of tools for addressing contextual detail and pattern if in the future we are to make effective choices.

us well. But education able to support and teach culturally mature capacities requires more. The essential tasks ahead for our species require
learnings incompatible with education's past definition. With modern
public education, for example, we've taken great care to keep moral
concerns out of the classroom—part of the separation of church and
state. But any kind of healthy future will require of all of us that we
confront increasingly complex ethical questions.

We can apply this same kind of more systemic discernment at larger
scales. Of particular importance, we need to apply it at the largest of
scales—to humanity as whole. Today our times are requiring us to ask
a particularly overarching Question of Referent: What in the future
must be our big-picture guide for making decisions? Here we've looked
at how no more important collective task exists today than fundamentally rethinking wealth and progress. In introducing what Creative Systems Theory calls the Dilemma of Trajectory, I described how taking
our Modern Age definition beyond its timeliness threatens to leave us
irreparably distanced from much that is ultimately most important to
us. And I've given particular attention to today's Crisis of Purpose and
proposed that its antidote lies in more directly engaging the question
of what could make our lives more purposeful. I could as well have said
that the antidote lies in recognizing and addressing today's newly systemic Question of Referent—and its necessarily more complete kind of
answer. Creative Systems Theory proposes that the concept of Cultural
Maturity provides that answer. Any act or idea consistent with the realization of culturally mature sensibilities becomes "true" in this now
most essential sense.

Capacitance:

Creative Systems Theory calls the second kind of Whole-Person/
Whole-System truth concept Capacitance. Capacitance describes a
system's overall capacity to take in and engage life. It addresses how
much of life's bigness we can tolerate. Think of a balloon. Capacitance
describes the size of the balloon, the "volume" of life a system can handle before things become too much.

While the concern of our first Whole-Person/Whole-System concept
was where culturally mature truth at its most basic might best be found,
Capacitance is more specifically quantitative. It is concerned with how

much truth—how much Aliveness—we can effectively manage. It is not about particular capacities—even general ones. It systemically circumscribes measures such as intelligence, skill, emotional maturity, power, adaptability, and sensitivity. Capacitance is about what at any point in time we are systemically capable of.

Capacitance is again a new kind of concept. Most immediately, it is new in being both more conscious and more embracing than what we have known. Historically, we've tended to think in terms of particular abilities or health parameters. It is also new—and radical—in that it demands Integrative Meta-perspective, and with this the whole of who we are, to effectively grasp and apply. This further kind of distinction is becoming increasingly essential. Measuring Capacitance more consciously and directly is not necessary if culturally mature understanding and action are not yet required. Split mind and body and we can measure intelligence well enough with an IQ test, and we can adequately evaluate the body with a physical exam. But with increasing frequency, today's circumstances demand that we address questions of possibility and capacity more systemically.

The concept of Capacitance again proves powerful at any systemic level. Certainly it is pertinent personally. As traditional cultural guideposts less and less define the structures of our daily lives, attention to Capacitance—both how much we have available and the Capacitance demands our lives make of us—becomes key to crafting our lives in ultimately healthy ways. It is rare in my work as a therapist that I don't at some point talk with clients about the importance of effectively managing Capacitance. The need for a concept like Capacitance comes into particularly high relief with the recognition of how, with today's ever more rush-rush existence, living over one's Capacitance has for many people become the norm. Attention to Capacitance gives us the feedback we need to live our personal lives in healthy and sustainable ways.[11]

The concept of Capacitance is also pertinent when it comes to leadership-related choices. If I wish to hire someone to fill a position for which the job description could change dramatically—as is so often

11 Colleague Mihaly Csikszentmihalyi described his concept of "flow" in what are essentially Capacitance terms. Flow becomes possible when the creative challenge is neither too great nor too small. (Mihaly Csikszentmihalyi, *Flow*, Harper, 2008.)

the case today—I don't want to base my decision purely on present skills. I am interested as much if not more in the person's ability to learn new skills, or even more generally, in how successfully the person handles complex and changing circumstances. I am interested in how much of the "stuff of life" the person can effectively hold and manage—their overall capacity to learn, act, relate, and grow.

With almost all of today's new challenges, from the most intimate to the global, we need to discern not just needed abilities, but what circumscribes them—how, and how generously and robustly, we are able to engage what the challenge asks of us. Our personal capacity for Whole-Person relationships—with friends or lovers, between parents and children, or leaders and followers—is ultimately a function of Capacitance. So is our ability as larger systems—communities, organizations, ethnicities, and countries—to relate with the new maturity our world increasingly demands.

The recognition that culturally mature understanding is itself Capacitance-dependent provides essential insight. This is not any more the case than what we find with previous major cultural change points. But being conscious of how this is so becomes newly pertinent if we are to successfully support Cultural Maturity's realization. When I choose participants for think-tank groups to address social issues, I carefully assess what level of Capacitance will be needed if we are to effectively take on the particular concern. I know that however skilled or clever I may be as a facilitator, if groups can't manage the needed level of engagement, we will fail at our task. Without sufficient Capacitance, culturally mature observations only create confusion. Importantly, the opposite is also the case. At a certain Capacitance, culturally mature insights become almost self-evident. While culturally mature perspective is impossible without sufficient Capacitance, it is also true that we don't have to advocate for culturally mature truths one by one. Rich dialogue helps. But in the end, we need only support the needed growth in Capacitance.

The new skills and capacities that I've described in introducing Cultural Maturity's changes help fill out Capacitance as a concept. Several in effect define Capacitance. Capacitance can be thought of as a system's capacity for responsibility. We can also define it as the amount of uncertainty a system can tolerate (noting that wallowing in uncertainty is a great way to diminish uncertainty). Equally well we can think of Capacitance as a measure of the amount of complexity a system can effectively embody (not forgetting the difference between systemic complexity and the merely complicated). Other new capacities that I've touched on—for example, getting beyond the either/or assumptions of times past or thinking more contextually—don't so directly describe Capacitance, but they are certainly Capacitance-dependent.

Another of those new capacities highlights what might initially seem an unwelcome aspect of this second Whole-Person/Whole-System notion. The concept of Capacitance confronts us immediately with the fact of inviolable limits. We like to believe that options are infinite and that people—and larger social systems—have unlimited potential. The concept of Capacitance reminds us that neither is the case. Our options are limited by how much our systemic vessel can hold without breaking.

At some level we know this is true. We don't have the same expectations of people at different ages. A caring parent does not inflict responsibilities on a five-year-old that require a ten-year-old's maturity. And a good teacher recognizes that while yes, "every child can learn," not all children can learn as well or at the same speed. It is the same with larger systems. Sometimes the growth a challenge might demand is beyond what a system is currently capable of engaging.

The concept of Capacitance is an essential tool if we are to judge effectively in a culturally mature reality. I've emphasized that CST has no problem with judgement. Indeed the theory highlights the importance of making judgments and getting better at doing so. But for judgement to benefit us, it must be based not on ideology, but on an accurate assessment of capacity. We commonly fall for one of two kinds of traps when it comes to judgement. We judge inaccurately—often on the basis of projections—with bias and bigotry the result. Or we conclude that judgement itself is a problem. The concept of Capacitance helps us make judgements that serve us.

The importance of using Capacitance in this way applies directly if we want to evaluate a person's ability to contribute in a culturally mature way. We can easily assume that people who believe things similar to ourselves are most advanced in their development. But, in fact, no particular background, gender, or temperament has an advantage when it comes to Cultural Maturity. Capacitance observations can offer surprising—indeed, enlightening—experiences. We can meet someone who we might previously have dismissed or even denigrated and suddenly realize that in fact they have quite high Capacitance. It is simply that their gifts manifest as a color or flavor of Capacitance that is significantly different from our own.[12]

It is important to recognize a basic relationship between Capacitance and polarization. When systems are confronted with challenges that exceed their Capacitance, they will polarize. This is a good thing. By reducing uncertainty and complexity, polarization works to protect systems from being further overwhelmed. As a therapist, I have found this recognition provides essential guidance in knowing how to be helpful. Often in the face of complex symptoms that are resistant to change, if a more conscious way to reduce the challenge to Capacitance can be found, the symptoms "magically" disappear.

The observation that systems tend to polarize when challenged to more than their available Capacitance sheds light on a unique danger we face today. In times past when polarization happened at a cultural level, it only increased polarization that was already part of consensus reality. The result might be war, but it was a familiar kind of war. Today, as polarization directly undermines the needed maturity of perspective, this sort of response becomes newly problematic. One of the great dangers we face today is that the easily overwhelming challenges we now confront—including those presented by Cultural Maturity–related changes—will stretch Capacitance beyond what we can tolerate. The resulting polarization and exacerbation of projection could distance us from the needed maturity of perspective just as such maturity has become imperative. I will return to this topic at the end of the chapter.

---

12 Observations in a previous footnote about the role of temporal context in making judgements point toward the importance of a concept like Capacitance if an evolutionary picture of history is to serve us. A good way to bring the dimension of time into our thinking is to ask whether at least the potential for the Capacitance needed to behave in more developed ways was present. With Nazi Germany, and as I have suggested, arguably slavery in the United States, it was. For a variety of reasons, people "chose" not to manifest that potential.

Polar Traps—and Polarity at Its Most Fundamental

Integrative Meta-perspective not only helps us rethink truth, it also helps us better appreciate where our truth claims stop short. Here again we've made a good start. I've contrasted Cultural Maturity with utopian and dystopian views of the future and spoken of how truths of an ideological sort reflect making particular crayons in the systemic box the whole of truth. I've observed how Patterning in Time concepts provide detail when it comes to more temporal compare-and-contrast distinctions. And I've just added how the concept of Capacitance, while a general notion, helps get at what all these various distinctions are ultimately measuring.

Creative Systems Theory also includes more specific tools for making wheat-from-chaff discernments. Observations about Capacitance and its relationship to polarization provide a good segue for one of the simplest, but also most ultimately powerful. I've described how a defining characteristic of culturally mature truth is that it "bridges" the polarized assumptions of times past. Thinking that reaches polarized conclusions is by its nature ideological. Creative Systems Theory's Creative Function provides a detailed framework for making such distinctions. But we can also draw on a more specific kind of "polar trap" language as a compact way to tease out different ways that our thinking can fail us.

This approach has its basis in previous insights about polarity at its most fundamental. I've described how contrasting polar positions are not about opposites in the sense that we tend to assume. At the least they reflect the particular kind of symmetry that I've observed in speaking of how polarities juxtapose more right-hand as opposed to more left-hand tendencies, characteristics that are more archetypally masculine versus more archetypally feminine. We've also seen how we can put the relationship more sparely. Polar positions juxtapose beliefs that identify most with difference/multiplicity and beliefs that identify most with connectedness/oneness. It is again a recognition that requires Cultural Maturity's cognitive reordering to fully grasp, but the perspective that results proves both conceptually powerful and immensely practical. Creative Systems Theory proposes that we can divide the various ways our thinking can miss the mark into three basic types of polar fallacies. It calls them Separation Fallacies, Unity Fallacies, and Compromise Fallacies. Put metaphorically, we can lose our way by falling off the right (more difference-defined) side of the systemic roadway, by falling off the left (more connectedness-defined) side, or by straddling the white line in the middle.

Separation Fallacies identify with the right-hand, archetypally masculine sensibilities. They equate truth with perceived fundamental distinctions such as between men and women, the material and the spiritual, the intellect and the emotions. And they give greatest value to the more creatively manifest side of the pertinent polarity (here, men, the material, and the intellect). Some common Separation Fallacy "half-truths": We are each wholly unique, individual. Experts have the answers. Final truth is what can be rationally articulated and objectively demonstrated. Human beings are wholly separate from nature and have rightful dominion over it. Change is a simple product of cause and effect.

Unity Fallacies identify with left-hand, archetypally feminine sensibilities. They give their allegiance to the softer, more creatively germinal aspects of creation. Related Unity Fallacy "half-truths" might include: In the end, we are all one (differences are ultimately irrelevant). The ordinary person knows best (better than leaders and institutions). Final truth is what we know from within. The task is to always live in accord with nature. Everything happens for a reason, even if that reason remains mysterious (it is all interrelated). Unity Fallacies argue against distinction and emphasize connectedness. They may claim a transcendence of polarity, but in fact they very specifically take sides—with the spiritual over the material, feelings over facts, the timeless over the specific.

Compromise Fallacies split the difference. This might seem to get us a bit closer, but if the task is culturally mature understanding, they fail us just as fundamentally. A few such Compromise Fallacy partial truths include: We are all different in our own ways ("different strokes for different folks"). There are lots of kinds of truth and each has its merits. Some Compromise Fallacies advocate a safe additive middle ground. Others argue correctly for multiple options, but give us nothing to help us beyond this accurate but meager observation—

they claim to address diversity but fail to address what makes differences different. Compromise Fallacies take us beyond black and white, but in the end replace it only with shades of gray. We often find them with postmodern thought.

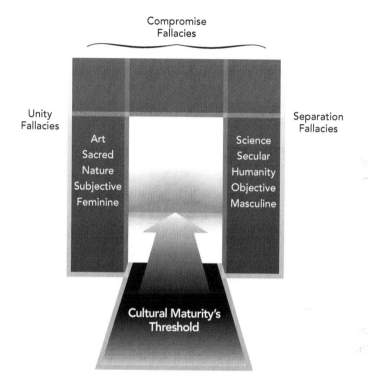

Fig. 5-2. Polar Fallacies

These are shorthand concepts. For starters, no one type of fallacy is as distinct from the others as the labels might suggest. For example, Unity Fallacies commonly carry a hidden Separation Fallacy, and Separation Fallacies similarly a hidden Unity Fallacy. A person who sees his own group as chosen and a conflicting group as evil succumbs to a Unity Fallacy with regard to his compatriots and a Separation Fallacy in relation to his adversaries.

In addition, there are in fact many versions of each type of fallacy. Some are going to be common with certain personality styles and specific views of the future, some with others. We can talk, for example, of multiple, very different kinds of Unity Fallacies. We often see a particularly spiritual sort of Unity Fallacy with advocates of New Age or back-to-the-land philosophies. But we also find very different Unity Fallacies with more fundamentalist religious beliefs that ally with "family values" and polarize against moral relativism and intellectual elites. Different yet are the more intellectual Unity Fallacies common in academic and liberal thought, which side with the underprivileged and polarize against conservatives and corporations. We can use the Creative Function to tease apart these different types of Unity Fallacy and to clarify why we predictably find them where we do.

The ability to recognize polar traps benefits us not just personally and conceptually, but also with efforts to address specific collective challenges more systemically. The immigration debate provides an example of an issue that today has become reflexively polarized. The language of polar fallacies can help us understand common polarized responses. We can think of the position of the political right as a Separation Fallacy—"build that wall." The views of the political left might seem less ideological—and they can be—but at the extreme they can come close to suggesting that the simple fact of boundaries is a problem—an obvious Unity Fallacy. And while Compromise Fallacy thinking that splits the difference might seem to move us forward in our thinking, building half a wall or letting in half the people would in the end just as much fail to provide useful solutions.[13]

The fact of polar fallacies in another way highlights how it is that while we may claim reasoned consideration as the basis for our conclusions, our beliefs tend to have as much to do with how we think as what we think. And these differences in how we think

---

13 I find the metaphor of a cell's semi-permeable membrane helpful for thinking about borders and immigration more creatively. Semi-permeable membranes make highly nuanced discernments with regard to what to let in based on what is most life-affirming for the cell. They are also highly sensitive to context. What may be most life-affirming for one cell may be very different from what is more life-affirming for another. And similarly, what is most supportive of life can be very different at different times and in different situations.

tend to be deep-seated. What we encounter when we confront one of our three basic kinds of fallacies may be a product only of momentary misunderstanding, but more often it will reflect underlying psychological/cognitive pattern. If we are vulnerable to polar traps, we will tend to fall for the same general sort of trap whatever the question.

We can use the concept of polar traps to further clarify how the various kinds of worldviews that I've contrasted with culturally mature understanding over the course of the book fall short. Both the more extreme of technology-focused utopian notions and the more tempered (or at least more camouflaged) views of Enlightenment philosophy, behaviorist psychology, and modern neuroscience reflect Separation Fallacy cognitive structures. And both the more extreme of New Age spiritually utopian views and the more tempered (or at least more camouflaged) views of philosophical romanticism and idealism, along with the more simplistic and ideological of liberal, environmental, and feminist beliefs, reflect Unity Fallacy cognitive structures. With systems thinking, we can similarly juxtapose the mechanistic (Separation Fallacy) assumptions of systems science and the all-is-one (Unity Fallacy) beliefs of systems views that might identify with more spiritual conclusions. And with current social/political polarization we find an increasingly extreme version of Separation Fallacy thinking with right-wing populist beliefs and ever more pure expressions of Unity Fallacy thinking with left-wing populist advocacy. I've noted how postmodern conclusions in their most basic different-strokes-for-different-folks manifestations are best thought of as Compromise Fallacies.[14]

Parts Work and Cultural Maturity's Necessary Cognitive Rewiring

There is one method that I find particularly powerful for supporting culturally mature truth. I call it simply Parts Work. I describe the approach in depth and provide numerous examples in my comprehensive work, *Creative Systems Theory*, but a few words

---

14 This is not always what we find with postmodern beliefs. In today's increasingly polarized world, often they join forces with left-wing populist Unity Fallacy thinking. We commonly find this in academia.

here help further fill out what makes culturally mature truth significant and different from truths of times past. If Parts Work is done well and we are ready for the stretch, the technique gives us almost no choice but to bring more mature and systemic perspective to bear.

CHAIRS REPRESENTING PARTS

CHAIR REPRESENTING
WHOLE-SYSTEM
PERSPECTIVE

In doing Parts Work, a person begins by envisioning various aspects of themselves—or perhaps aspects of a question that concerns them—like characters in a play. Leading from his or her Whole-Person/Whole-System perspective chair, the person engages the various parts set in chairs around the room in conversation, moving back and forth between the Whole-Person chair and the various parts. My job is to facilitate these conversations. Parts Work can also be done with more than one person to address larger cultural issues.

The result can be striking. Talking about culturally mature truth in terms of holding the whole box of crayons of our systemic complexity or practicing the various new capacities that Integrative Meta-perspective makes possible can take us a long way. But Parts Work's more "hands-on" methodology gets us there with a directness that is hard to achieve by other means.

Parts Work follows three cardinal rules. Together these rules address Integrative Meta-perspective and its implications in a way that is quite precise. Each rule informs a particular aspect of culturally mature understanding.

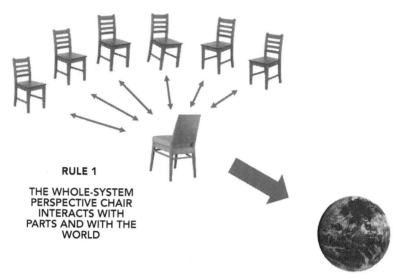

RULE 1

THE WHOLE-SYSTEM PERSPECTIVE CHAIR INTERACTS WITH PARTS AND WITH THE WORLD

The first rule: *Only the Whole-Person/Whole-System Perspective Chair Interacts with Parts and with the World.* It is the Whole-Person chair (or the Whole-System chair with larger cultural issues) that provides the leadership with Parts Work. This rule makes doing Parts Work an exercise for practicing culturally mature authority—in oneself and in the world.

RULE 2

PARTS DON'T INTERACT WITH THE WORLD

The second rule follows from the first: *Parts Don't Interact with the World.* A person doing Parts Work quickly recognizes that engaging the world from parts, while it is what most people do the larger portion of the time, produces limited and limiting results. People also come to recognize that ideological beliefs—whether political, religious, or those of competing belief systems within their particular professions—involve parts taking over and acting as if they have a relationship with the world.

RULE 3
PARTS DON'T INTERACT
WITH EACH OTHER

The third cardinal rule: *Parts Don't Interact with Each Other*. The recognition that parts don't talk to parts can take a bit longer to grasp, but it is ultimately just as critical. We can think of much in the internal struggles of daily life as crosstalk between competing parts. And the implications are just as significant collectively. Parts talking to parts is what has us easily confuse moderation or compromise with culturally mature perspective, and ideological beliefs of the less extreme sort often have their roots in parts talking to parts. Creative Systems Theory describes how we can understand the back and forth between competing worldviews over the course of history as a similar sort of conversation between systemic parts.

The result when a person follows these cardinal rules is a kind of "cognitive rewiring." Wires are cut between both parts and the world, and between parts. And at the same time, people strengthen the wires that run between themselves and the world, and also between themselves and their diverse and variously creative and contributing parts. Key to the power of the Parts Work approach is that the person doesn't need to be conscious of why it is working. Get the wiring right and culturally mature understanding and culturally mature leadership capacities are natural results.

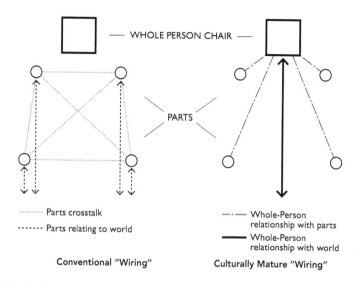

Fig. 5-3. Cultural Maturity's Cognitive Rewiring

As a therapist, I use Parts Work to help people address internal conflicts, explore Whole-Person relationship, and develop culturally mature leadership capacities. In think tank settings, I use it to address conflicting societal beliefs and to help people grasp how ideological conclusions that might seem incompatible may reflect aspects of a needed larger systemic picture.

Parts Work can also be used to engage overarching questions more systemically. In *Creative Systems Theory*, I offer an example that is particularly pertinent to our task with this book. I describe how the approach can help reconcile the most ultimate and timeless of polarities—that which divides the material and the spiritual, science and religion. Parts Work, when done well, challenges the assumptions equally of someone who identifies with more scientific or more religious conclusions. The way it does further highlights how culturally mature perspective is new in a fundamental sense. It also provides good illustration of the power of Parts Work.

Someone of more scientific bent doing Parts Work is likely, at least initially, to assume that a part that thinks rationally and scientifically appropriately sits in the Whole-Person/Whole-System chair. This is not an unreasonable assumption given where the person has often most found significance. But it is not too long before the person sees that there are many concerns, and concerns of no small importance, particularly in one's personal life—such as purpose or love—where this part is limited in what it has to contribute. Eventually, the person comes to recognize how more than this part is needed not just for making good personal life choices, but for the most filled out and creative kind of science.

Something very similar tends to happen for people who identify with more spiritual sensibilities. This may be an individual with quite traditional religious beliefs, a person with more humanistic "spiritual but not religious" tendencies, or someone of more New Age bent. Commonly the person will assume that spiritual truth appropriately sits in the Whole-Person/Whole-System chair. Again, for them, this is not an unreasonable conclusion. But if the person of more spiritual/religious inclination works long enough, they recognize in a similar way that having spiritual truth sit in the Whole-Person/Whole-System chair in our time leads to problems. An all too common result is poorly thought-out life choices and unsuccessful relationships. It turns out that in a well-lived life—a spiritual life in the best sense—the more manifest parts of existence are as important as the essences. Eventually, the person may realize that holding the spiritual more systemically in this way will be key not just to making good everyday choices, but to the most full and creative relationship to spiritual experience.

In doing Parts Work, the chairs that advocate for aspects of larger truths—whether personal truths or truths of a more social or even more philosophical/existential sort—each in important ways add to the Whole-Person/Whole-System perspective chair's reflections. But they function at most as consultants. When we miss this fact, ultimately unhelpful—indeed dangerous—specifically ideological conclusions result. With Parts Work, people confront this recognition not just as some abstract conclusion, but personally and immediately. Living from the Whole-Person/Whole-System chair is the defining task with culturally mature leadership—whether in our personal lives or more broadly. We can think of doing so as what ultimately defines today's needed new common sense.

Parts Work provides a further way to put Cultural Maturity's changes in historical perspective. It starts with the basic recognition that the polarity-based beliefs of times past, however the polarity was depicted, represented a parts-talking-to-parts relationship. Prior to now (at a cultural level) there has simply not been the option of a Whole-Person/Whole-System leadership chair. The Creative Function maps such parts-talking-to-parts cognitive dynamics through history.

I've previously described how both the way we experience polar qualities and the way polar opposites relate to one another evolve in characteristic ways over the course of any formative process. Historically in the West we see a progression from complementary relationships like the intertwined snakes of the Greek caduceus in Early-Axis, to more clearly antagonistic juxtapositions as with Christian representations of good and evil in Middle-Axis, and finally more cleanly cleaved polar concepts such as objective and subjective with Late-Axis belief. Here we add simply that in each case, if we were doing Parts Work, we would experience the juxtaposition as a parts-talking-to-parts conversation.

A person could object that I must be missing something with my emphasis on this basic two-part dynamic and my claim that Integrative Meta-perspective is something new. Polar relationships have often been described historically in terms of three aspects—as with classical Chinese philosophy where we have not just yin and yang, but also the Tao (the way) and with the Christian trinity. We frequently encounter a related kind of three-part picture with depictions of psychological dynamics—as with Freud's id, ego, and superego. The essential recognition is that the third element in these various depictions, while significant, represents something wholly different than Integrative Meta-perspective (of either the personal or cultural development sort). Rather, it reflects the more limited kind of reconciling truth that comes with a right and timely creative relationship between polar extremes. It is a product of this kind of parts-talking-to-parts dynamic.

We find confirmation for this essential distinction in the observation that right and timely balance points in this sense change depending on the stage in the pertinent developmental dynamic. We can think of the third option in any traditional triad as like a slider proceeding from left to right between extremes over the course of any formative process. This includes both personal and cultural development.[15] Integrative

---

15 We can see this by contrasting how psychoanalysis and traditional Buddhist thought depict the correct fate for the ego. Each defines the term

Meta-perspective of either the cultural or personal development sort—what we find with Parts Work when we occupy the Whole-Person/Whole-System leadership chair—provides a fundamentally different kind of vantage and experienced reality.

Parts Work offers a simple way to think about a truth-related observation suggested earlier that is essential to effectively making our way in these easily confusing times. I've described Cultural Maturity's new picture as at once more complex and more straightforward, even "ordinary," than what it replaces. Ways of understanding that today become highly visible or attract significant numbers of followers tend to be ideological. Put in Parts Work terms, they are going to reflect "parts talking to the world" or "parts talking to parts." We experience ideas that consistently reflect the perspective of the Whole-Person/Whole-System chair and avoid polar traps more as common sense. They are as yet rare. They can't continue to be.[16]

"ego" in generally similar ways. But in keeping with its Late-Axis cultural origins, psychoanalysis views the psychotherapeutic task as strengthening the ego (pushing the slider to the right). In contrast, in keeping with its Early-Axis cultural roots, classical Buddhism sees the task as transcending the ego (pushing the slider to the left). I've observed that the term "ego" today gets used differently by different schools of psychological thought. Most often the implication is what I've noted here—the third option in a traditional triad. But as with what I described with the concept of "self" in the previous chapter, we can also find the term applied in ways that begin to approach identity in the sense that results with Integrative Meta-perspective, at least with such perspective's more limited manifestation in individual psychological development.

16 Parts Work as described here represents a major contribution—and step forward—in the practice of psychotherapy. It actively draws on intelligence's multiple aspects (unusual, though it is not alone in this regard); in contrast to most more traditional methodologies, it places the final authority not with the therapist as interpreter, but in the hands of the person in the Whole-Person leadership chair; and while there are other approaches that work actively with parts (I think in particular of Jacob Moreno's Psychodrama, Roberto Assagioli's Psychosynthesis, and Hal and Sidra Stone's Voice Dialogue), the three cardinal rules mean that Parts Work as I have described it supports culturally mature growth in a way that other methods at best do indirectly. Of particular importance in this regard is how only the

Ideology and Regression

I've promised to return to the topic of my most recent book, *Perspective and Guidance for a Time of Deep Discord*. Besides highlighting one of our time's most pressing concerns, it helps further fill out how our times are challenging us to grasp the ultimately systemic nature of truths of all sorts. I wrote the book because of great concern I feel for our times' growing social and political polarization. Over the last thirty years, we've seen such reactive polarization become ever more pronounced and people's voices becoming ever more shrill. Of particular pertinence to this book's contribution, extreme polarization makes culturally mature understanding essentially impossible.

A couple of insights related to today's extreme polarization tie directly to this chapter's truth-related reflections. The first concerns the question of just what we are seeing with these circumstances. In a further way the question brings attention to the basic observation that we need to focus on cognitive mechanisms if beliefs are to make sense. The second turns to the essential question of just why we see what we do. My answer ties to truth-related observations I've made with regard to the concept of Capacitance, and also to earlier descriptions of the dynamics of Transition.

Let's start with the "what we see" insight. What we witness with today's increasing political and social polarization brings us back to the now familiar recognition that our conclusions tend to have less to do with what we think than how we think. Ultimately they are about something more basic even than collections of beliefs and values, what people refer to with a term like "worldview"—though that gets us a bit closer. What we witness reflects psychological patterns, or more precisely, patterns of cognitive organization. It is not so much that belief is creating polarization, than that polarity's role in how we think is creating polarized belief.

---

person in the Whole-Person leadership chair (not the therapist/facilitator) talks with parts, something not found with any other method that I am aware of. The Parts Work approach also has interesting implications for the training of therapists. While it requires well-developed culturally mature capacities on the part of the practitioner, it doesn't demand complex understanding of psychodynamics and unconscious processes. For a person who is ready, it is not that hard to teach.

Most people will find the notion that social/political polarization has more to do with our cognitive mechanisms than the real complexities of policy surprising. We tend to think of our opinions in terms of rationally arrived-at conclusions. And the media tends to take at face value that what a person says is generally what he or she means, or at the least that the words adequately reflect what drives the person's concerns. But the recognition that we are dealing with underlying cognitive patterns is key. It is critical to making sense of why getting beyond polarization can be so difficult and also to why efforts at civil discourse so often fail. And if the concept of Cultural Maturity is accurate, it is essential to understanding what is needed going forward.

The particulars of belief can in fact be products of reasoned consideration. And beliefs can be influenced by numerous external factors—where we live (for example, urban versus rural), the family we grow up in, or the unique challenges our particular life may present. But when belief takes the form of ideology, we are seeing psychological pattern. We can think of these patterns as "ecological niches" in the makeup of our psyches. Different kinds of social narratives fit most comfortably into particular cognitive niches.

Some of the best evidence that today's extreme social and political polarization has less to do with what we think than how we think can be found in the common intractableness of people's opinions. We tend to assume that when people have views different from our own, the appropriate response is to engage in reasoned discussion and debate. But in fact debate rarely changes anyone's mind. As often the result is positions becoming even more entrenched.

We find further evidence in how often issues that eventually become highly polarized are not thought of in partisan terms when they first come to the public's attention. This was the case, for example, with both climate change and health care reform. There were no obvious sides to the climate change debate when the evidence first came to light. And the approach on which Obamacare was initially modeled was Republican Mitt Romney's plan in Massachusetts.

We find an important additional kind of evidence in the common closeness of elections. If voting were based on the perceived intelligence of a candidate and his or her ideas, much more often than we do we would see general agreement as to which candidate is the most qualified. Instead, elections are most often won by a few percentage points, or less. This is what we would predict if we are dealing not just with differences of opinion, but opposite polarized cognitive patterns. Pushed to extremes, polarities split fifty-fifty, like two sides of a coin. One of the best ways to win an election if you are not really qualified is to create controversy and polarization. Because polar opposites tend to split about evenly, you should then be able to get something close to half of the vote.

Another place we find evidence is in the almost inverse relationship that exists between how informed a person is and the likelihood that he or she will have strong views. If surety was a product of how thoroughly topics had been researched, we would expect the opposite. But commonly we find the most strident views and the most lengthy pronouncements with people who in fact know the least and have least to offer to a real conversation. Less information more quickly aligns with cognitive patterns. More information risks creating internal dissonance.

It turns out that if we have sufficiently nuanced conceptual tools available to us, we can make pretty accurate predictions about the ideological beliefs that we will encounter by teasing apart psychological structures and patterns.[17] What we can then predict is underlying values more than particular opinions, but this kind of observation can prove immensely useful. At the least, it helps make sense of otherwise confusing results—such as how people can have views that would seem not in their best interest or how we so often find strange-bedfellow alliances. It also helps us appreciate what the more encompassing kind of understanding that comes with culturally mature systemic perspective involves and just what it requires of us.

The second topic is equally worthy of our attention. I gave the *Perspective and Guidance* book the subtitle: *"Why We See Such Extreme Social and Political Polarization—and What We Can Do About It."* Interestingly, I have an easier time identifying solutions than confidently providing explanation. In the book, I describe in detail the backsliding over the last twenty or thirty years that I've briefly noted here. I also admit that it is not fully clear to me just why we are seeing it. But

---

17 See the Creative Systems Personality Typology in Chapter Seven.

uncertainties acknowledged, the question of why we witness what we do is definitely important. Consequences could be very different with different answers. And depending on our answer, what is being asked of us could also be very different. With several explanations, major changes—at least in the short term—may not be needed. But there are also reasons to think we may be dealing with dynamics of a more fundamental sort.

It is quite possible that the extreme polarization we witness today is not of great concern. It could be a product simply of the common two-steps-forward-one-step-back nature of societal change. It is also possible that what we see could follow from dynamics more particular to our time but which still have familiar antidotes. Today's extreme views might reflect momentary regression in the face of today's many highly demanding challenges. I've described how it is in the nature of human systems that they will often polarize and regress when confronted with demands that threaten to overwhelm them—when they are pushed beyond their available Capacitance. If the challenges are temporary and the overwhelm is not that great, patience and perspective—at least if we can avoid making destructive choices in response to being overwhelmed—should be all that is needed to take care of things.

But what we are seeing could also be a consequence of more ultimately overwhelming challenges and with them regression of a more pronounced—and less easily addressed—sort. Many of today's critical concerns—for example, globalization, climate change, job loss through automation, the dramatic changes of the information revolution, the growing gap between the world's haves and have-nots, and the loss of familiar cultural guideposts in so many areas of our lives (from generally agreed-upon moral codes to clearly defined national and religious allegiances)—are more specifically new and could result in overwhelm of a particularly severe sort. It is important to recognize that regressive dynamics over recent decades have spanned the globe. We see them in the growing prevalence of authoritarian rule in fledgling democracies. We also find them with the rising tide of fundamentalism in the Islamic East. If what we witness is primarily a product of such more deeply demanding and often global dynamics, successfully moving forward could be considerably more difficult. Indeed, what effectively moving forward asks may be more than we are capable of.

Importantly, there is an observation hidden in these descriptions with particular pertinence to the legitimacy of hope. If it is accurate, while it doesn't make things easier, it does alter the possible implications. Aspects of this easily overwhelming picture—for example, the loss of familiar guideposts in many areas of our lives—may be products of Cultural Maturity–related changes. The demands that come with Cultural Maturity's "growing up"—including taking greater responsibility in our choices, better tolerating life's real uncertainties and complexities, and more effectively dealing with real limits—require that we face realities that before now we could not have tolerated. If such demands are playing a major role in current circumstances, this would further increase what our times require of us—considerably. But it would also increase the likelihood that we can get through these difficult times. It would mean that what we are feeling overwhelmed by may be at least in part what in the end will be required to save us. Today's backsliding could be part of an awkward in-between time in a predicted developmental process.

In the book I note kinds of evidence beyond just the nature of the challenges we face that support the idea that Cultural Maturity's changes may play a role in what we are seeing. I describe, for example, how the degree of absurdity that we often find today can be thought of as evidence. (I reference the concept of Transitional Absurdity.) In addition, I observe how the fact that today we find polarization not just between historically common competing forces, but between alternative extreme populist ideologies is consistent with what the concept of Cultural Maturity would predict. (I describe how it is something we should expect to find with the peak of Transition.)

At this point, two recognitions are key. First, whatever their origins, today's extreme social and political polarization directly puts us at risk. The critical nature of so many of the challenges that we now confront means that such deep divisions present real dangers. Second, whatever the cause, what is being called for is ultimately the same—the ability to understand our worlds in more mature and encompassing ways. This is the case even if the challenge is only to weather the effects of more particular stressors. But it is particularly true if Cultural Maturity's demands are playing a significant role in what we see. Specific policy approaches could have an impact. For example, anything that begins to address today's growing economic disparities could lessen populist tensions. And, in the short term, we may get away with simply finding ways to better get along. But with time, the need for the kind of more integrative change that comes with Cultural Maturity's cognitive reordering should become inescapable.

A simple lesson provides the structure in *Perspective and Guidance for a Time of Deep Discord*. It also offers basic guidance when beliefs of any sort become polarized. In times past when we encountered polarized positions and partisan advocacy, our task was obvious and unquestioned. We assumed that there were only two options and that our job was to figure out which one was right and fight for it. As we look to the future, polarization has very different implications. It alerts us to the fact that we have yet to ask the hard questions that ultimately need to be addressed. When we succeed at asking the larger questions, we recognize that there have always been more than just two sides. We also see that while each traditional side may hold a piece of the truth, neither side by itself, nor just some averaging of positions, can get us where we need to go. Moving forward effectively will require bringing greater maturity—and more encompassing perspective—to how we make sense of our worlds and the truths on which we base our choices. The book specifically addresses an array of issues that commonly evoke polarized responses in our time—climate change, health care reform, abortion, race and gender relations, immigration, and more. With each I demonstrate how more systemic perspective is possible. I also emphasize that when we are up to the challenge, the results can seem straightforward—in the end, like common sense.

CHAPTER SIX

The Critical Role of Creative Context in Ideas that Can Serve Us Going Forward

In Chapter One's brief listing of new capacities that accompany Cultural Maturity's changes, I ended with "better understanding how events happen in a context." When we step beyond history's shared parental absolutes and a time's more particular ideological beliefs, we confront how dramatically truth is contextual. What works to make things more depends on when and where we look.

We don't need to engage human systems to recognize such living contextual relativity. The realities of a bear, a bee, or a bat are going to be very different from one another. And while we might assume human understanding to be superior, in fact if I were any of these other creatures, their view of the world would be more useful, and thus in effect most true.

But appreciating contextual relativity does have particular importance when it comes to ourselves. At first, such relativity can be difficult to grasp. We are more used to thinking of our truths as once-and-for-all and absolute. Or if we do acknowledge the role of context, we are likely to stop with postmodern, anything-goes assumptions. Integrative Meta-perspective makes contextual relativity obvious. It also invites us to engage it with a depth and complexity that has not before been an option. Ideas that can help us understand with the needed contextual sophistication are in the end, again, necessarily radical, new in a fundamental sense. But it is a now familiar kind of newness. One of the most important consequences of Cultural Maturity's cognitive reordering is that it allows us to make highly precise discernments that are precise exactly because they take contextual nuance into account.

We can think of this result in terms of either of the primary ways I've spoken of Integrative Meta-perspective and the power of a creative frame.

We can understand the theory's ability to address contextual nuance in terms of the role of polarity in formative process. In examining the Dilemma of Differentiation, I described how creatively framed systemic perspective lets us think in ways that simultaneously embrace difference and connectedness. Creative Systems Theory, by bringing detail to how difference and connectedness interplay in different ways at various times and places, provides a way to delineate contextual pattern in the workings of human systems. In a similar way we can understand the theory's ability to address context in terms of how Integrative Meta-perspective provides a more direct connection with intelligence's multiple aspects. When we draw on the whole of intelligence's multiplicity and do so in needed more conscious and integrative ways, the fact that truth is contextual becomes obvious.

We can think of Creative Systems Theory's framework for understanding purpose, change, and interrelationship as a set of tools for making culturally mature context-specific discernments. This accomplishment should now make basic sense with Patterning in Time notions. Patterning in Time concepts emphasize that culturally mature decision-making requires being keenly attentive to temporal context. While at a cultural level sensitivity to one's own temporal context has always been important, in times past it came with being embedded in one's cultural time—like water to a fish. Integrative Meta-perspective is needed if we are to consciously and deeply understand ourselves in the context of time. And certainly it is necessary if we are to appreciate the temporal contexts of others.

Patterning in Space notions address here-and-now contextual relativity. They make a similarly more dynamic and nuanced kind of discernment for systemic differences at a specific point in time—for example, between domains in culture, academic disciplines, groups with different ideological leanings, or individuals with differing personality styles. We've made a start here in observing how polarized positions can have us reach wholly different kinds of conclusions. The Creative Systems Personality Typology provides the most developed set of Patterning in Space distinctions in the theory.

Patterning in Time reflections in Chapter Three provided a good first look at the powerful—and radical—results that come when we bring Integrative Meta-perspective and a creative frame to questions of context. We saw, for example, how doing so lets us understand history in ways that are more dynamic, in terms of underlying sensibilities, values, and worldviews. We also saw how a creative frame helps us get beyond just the "what" of circumstances and get at the "why.' Most often when people claim to be addressing why—whether on the evening news or with a history lecture—more accurately they are stringing together a sequence of whats. Patterning in Time and Patterning in Space concepts help bring detail to the particulars of experience, but they are always too about why experience organizes in the specific ways that it does at different times and places.

Creative Systems Theory's approach to understanding contextual relativity is highly unusual in that it addresses both temporal distinctions and here-and-now differences. It is unique as far as I know in conceptually linking these two kinds of contextual relativity. In times past, if we've acknowledged contextual differences at all, we've considered these two kinds of distinctions to be wholly different concerns. I've noted how Creative Systems Theory uses the same creative language when making Patterning in Time and Patterning in Space distinctions. The link is not just one of nomenclature. Again we confront how what we think is a reflection of the cognitive structures with which we are doing the thinking. With Integrative Meta-perspective—and specifically with the application of a creative frame—we find that a related kind of mapping helps us understand both change and interrelationship in human systems.

The way Creative Systems Theory is able to address contextual relativity again shines a light on how a creative frame makes possible ideas that are at once more complex and simpler than what they replace. One of the most striking consequences when applying CST patterning concepts is how often they make it possible to capture highly complicated phenomena in quite simple terms. The idea of a new Fundamental Organizing Concept that underlies truths of all sorts reflects this contribution at its most basic. Creative Systems patterning concepts add a further critical step. By inviting us to recognize relationships within multifaceted and multilayered concerns—and often even between dynamics that might at first seem totally unrelated—they produce ways of mapping experience that can be remarkably elegant in their simplicity.

Here I'll first touch a bit further on Patterning in Time distinctions to provide additional insight into the depth and importance of the kinds of discernments they make possible. I'll then turn to Patterning in Space distinctions with particular emphasis on the Creative Systems Personality Typology's unique contribution.[1]

More Patterning in Time

We've made a solid start with Patterning in Time distinctions. In Chapter Two, I described how we can understand Cultural Maturity in terms of the evolution of cultural narrative—the stories we've told about how things work. In Chapter Three, we looked at how we can apply a creative frame to understanding human developmental processes of all sorts—a simple creative act, individual human development, change in a relationship, or the evolution of culture. And in Chapter Five, I described how the evolution of belief could be understood in terms of the how intelligence manifests at different points in human formative processes.

Such observations are useful not just for understanding the past, but also for making good decisions in the present. For example, prior to the second Iraq War, leaders in the U.S. assumed that liberation by American forces would be celebrated by the Iraqi people and that all would be well if the dictatorial structures of Saddam Hussein could be replaced by more Western-style democratic institutions. An appreciation for the fact that the larger part of modern-day Iraq exists in a cultural time roughly analogous to late medieval Europe would have made clear that neither expectation was warranted. Involvement in Afghanistan was arguably more justified, but given that modern-day Afghanistan exists in a time closer to eighth- or ninth-century Europe, related expectations there (and really expectations of success of any significant kind) were even less warranted.

I've made reference to how we find a dangerous failure to acknowledge temporal context today with populist thinking on both the Left and the

---

1 The recognition of the importance of context has notable antecedents. It was foreshadowed, for example, in Immanuel Kant's admonition that we must not confuse our thoughts with reality. More recently it is a key theme with the social constructivist thread in postmodern thought. For instance, we hear it hinted at in the familiar refrain from general semantics that "the map is not the territory." But most often, again, we run into the familiar postmodern aversion to detail and overarching perspective. One exception is the broad acceptance over the last century of the ideas of developmental psychology when it comes to temporal differences in individual human thought and perception.

Right. From the Left, too often we encounter a naive judging of the past in terms of the values and beliefs of the present. From the Right, we often see denial that culture indeed evolves—and continues to evolve. Neither stance can get us where we need to go.

In *Creative Systems Theory*, I look in depth at how Patterning in Time distinctions provide insight with regard to a wide array of topics. With some of these topics, most people would not recognize that there are differences to observe, much less recognizable patterns. This is particularly the case with topics where more left-hand, archetypally feminine characteristics play a significant role. For example, I examine how time is experienced differently at various points in any formative process and how these differences manifest with different stages in history. (It turns out that time itself is relative in time.) I also examine how the way we experience the body changes with each creative stage, a fact reflected historically not just in how we have interpreted experience at different times, but also in how we have thought about what it means to have a body and to heal bodily ailments. I also describe how music and art have identifiable common characteristics at each cultural stage.

For this chapter I will include Patterning in Time observations that pertain to a couple of spheres—architecture and philosophy—that help fill out this approach in particularly informative ways. The history of architecture has much to teach because of how directly it brings together more left-hand and more right-hand influences. The progression it describes is as much sculptural as technical, and as much spiritual as practical. Looking at philosophy through a creative lens brings nuance to a pursuit that traditionally we have thought of only in dry, rational terms—and in the process helps bring it to life.

Architecture and the Developmental "Anatomy" of History

As a sculptor, I've found myself intrigued by how architecture's monumental physical expressions, like the best of sculpture, reflect the ways we have held reality at the time and place of their creation. In modern times, people often assume that architecture's changes through history have been products largely of invention, of what we have become capable of building. More accurately, particular shapes move us when they speak from how we are coming to experience and shape reality as a whole. The evolution of architecture, particularly architecture that is regarded by the people of its time as in some way sacred or special, makes a particularly fascinating lens through which to observe culture's creative metamorphosis. The following observations are adapted from *The Creative Imperative*. Similarities noted not only cut across cultural traditions within particular cultures, they reflect patterns found everywhere at parallel periods in culture:

In earliest prehistory (early Pre-Axis), the most common ritual dwelling was the earth itself. The "medicine" of early Stone Age people—drawings and ritual objects—has been found most often in the deep recesses of caves. It was apparently these caves, and such sites as sacred wells and burial mounds, that were the most common places for the shaman's "discourses" with the primordial powers of nature. Sculpturally, the sacred forms in this most archetypally feminine of periods were spherical containers and gentle mounds.

With the beginnings of Early-Axis sensibility, attention began to shift upward. Ritual spaces increasingly became ritual structures, and these structures specifically places for conferring with the heavens. The Neolithic stone circles of Europe provide some of the earliest examples,[2] while the pyramids of Egypt and Mesoamerica are somewhat later, and the temples of early Greece and the ritual dwellings of the classical East—Buddhist stupas, Hindu temples—somewhat later still. The architectural mass remains in secure juxtaposition to the earth's belly, but now there is a clear verticality. Worshippers stand below and gaze upward.

---

2 Every few years a new theory appears that purports to explain the "mystery" of Stonehenge. Such theories tend to focus on particular uses. We find more basic explanation in how Stonehenge's form reflected emerging possibility in human evolution. It is this that made it a sacred site, whatever particular activities might be carried out within its structure.

Approaching Middle-Axis times, places of worship increasingly reflect an equal structural affinity with Above and Below. The domes of the Byzantine period very nearly balance in their upward might the weight of the foundation and sanctuary beneath. In the uplifted towers and high rounded arches of Romanesque architecture, we see the first gestures toward ascendant preeminence, an emphasis made more fully manifest in the last centuries of Middle-Axis culture in Europe with the Gothic cathedral's surging buttresses and poetic spires.

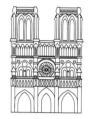

With the beginnings of Late-Axis culture, we find two important architectural themes. The first is the continuation of upward movement. The second is the secularization of the ascendant. The most powerful gods of industrial high culture reside in the material realm, not the church. The culminating form of this period is the skyscraper. With its glass and steel purity, it is a perfect monument to objectivity and rational abstraction.

With Transitional times, we've taken one further step. The skyscraper continues to have an important place, but it is joined by an even more ascendant image: the spacecraft. The spacecraft is a ritual dwelling in which humans not only contemplate the heavens, they inhabit them.

Today we see the beginnings of additional steps. The postmodern sensibility in architecture directly questions Late-Axis orthodoxies. And in keeping with the idea that earlier stages might have lessons to teach, it makes at least a start at entertaining aesthetics from earlier times. The worst of postmodern architecture presents little more than a hodgepodge of influences. But the best can bring together diverse aesthetics in truly striking and inspiring ways. I think for example of Jørn Utzon's Sydney Opera House and Frank Gehry's Guggenheim Museum in Bilbao. I look forward to what more the future may bring.

The History of Philosophy

One of Patterning in Time's most provocative contributions is the way it helps us put truths of all sorts in historical perspective. We can use a creative frame to help us delineate how truths tied to particular realms of understanding have evolved through time—religious truth, scientific truth, artistic truth, or our conclusions about government, education, or medicine. In these pages, we've begun to see how it can also be used to address truth itself—just what makes truth true—the endeavor captured most broadly by philosophy.

Creative Systems Theory starts out by alerting us to limits inherent in philosophy's approach. Philosophy, even when interpreted very broadly as here, means ideas that can be verbally articulated and put into some rational form (even if their focus is the nonrational). Thus, while philosophy claims to be about truth, the perspective from which it views truth often limits what it is capable of grasping. But once we recognize philosophy's limitations, philosophical truth provides a valuable window. At the least it is representative of broader understanding. And because it tends toward verbal descriptions and logical analysis, philosophy is more amenable to brief synopsis (ignoring for the moment the fact that philosophers are rarely brief) than, say, the historical "beliefs" of art, architecture, or religion.

The Creative Function provides a crude but provocative way to "map" the history of philosophy. Besides applying the Creative Function's general evolutionary picture, such mapping draws on a key recognition that mirrors previous observations in this book. We can think of philosophical tradition as having left and right hands (or at least traditions that lean variously to the left or right). Philosophy refers to these two fundamental currents in a variety of ways—the transcendental as opposed to the empirical, the approach of the idealist or the romantic as opposed to the positivist or the materialist. Each at times flows into the other, but the simplification supports understanding. Jean Gebser described the situation this way in *The Ever-Present Origin*: "Idealists and materialists are like two children on a seesaw who have been teetering back and forth for two thousand years."

The more left-hand current includes thinkers such as Plato and philosophers of more religious bent who believe that what we can ultimately most rely on is inner experience, whether mental or spiritual. The more right-hand current includes thinkers who in one way or another believe we rely ultimately (or at least most usefully) on our senses, such as the early natural philosophers, Aristotle, and most of modern science. It is commonly observed in philosophical circles that we can understand the whole of Western thought as following in the tradition either of Plato or Aristotle.

Creative Systems Theory expands on this recognition by applying the observation that polarities organize creatively. The history of ideas becomes a chronicling of the diverse ways in which this two-handed interplay has been perceived through time, and from different perspectives at particular points in time. If nothing else, this approach offers the possibility of synopsis and an antidote to that common lack of brevity in philosophical writings.

Two basic, now familiar change processes shape this philosophical trek through time. The first is that gradual shift from a more left-hand, archetypally feminine emphasis to a more right-hand, archetypally masculine emphasis. Left-handed cosmologies predominate in earliest cultural periods, while more right-handed worldviews come to the fore as we have moved toward the present. The second is how creative stages—Pre-Axis, Early-Axis, Middle-Axis, Late-Axis—give each hand identifiable characteristics depending on when it manifests. There is also a further change dynamic more specific to our time—the way Transitional dynamics are calling into question the conclusions of each of these traditions. Twentieth-century pragmatist Richard Rorty put it this way: "Both traditions are now in a period of doubt about their own status. Both are living between a repudiated past and a dimly seen post-philosophical future."[3]

The following briefest of overviews is adapted from *Creative Systems Theory*. Descriptions are highly (even absurdly) abridged. I will mention thinkers and belief systems without great elaboration. Readers may find some familiarity with philosophical thought's key figures and traditions to be helpful, but the most important recognitions concern the suggested underlying patterns.

---

3 I include Rorty among figures whose ideas at least begin to engage Cultural Maturity's threshold. (Richard Rorty, *Consequences of Pragmatism*, University of Minnesota Press, 1982.)

Many people would not consider where we must start philosophy, given that tribal (Pre-Axis) beliefs precede written language. But the animistic assumptions of Pre-Axis times do produce a consistent kind of worldview. I've described how experience in tribal societies is defined almost exclusively by left-hand sensibilities. It is not that right-hand elements are denied; rather, simply, they are not yet strongly present. All is seen as connected—tribe, nature, spirit, time—and these connections define truth. People may assume more right-hand and left-hand roles—a tribal chief's duties are more "secular" than those of a shaman. But differences manifest within an almost entirely unitary holding of experience.

While the cosmologies of civilization's early rise (Early-Axis) more overtly acknowledge both hands of truth, the left hand, as I've observed, retains dominance. The magical and mythic beliefs of ancient Egypt, the Incas and Aztecs, classical India and China, or Olympian Greece each gave primary emphasis to the archetypally feminine. Plato's philosophy belongs in this left-hand tradition, though he conceived of truth's left hand more in terms of mind than spirit. In Plato's cave, external reality is a play of shadows cast by internal essences—the "forms" or "ideas." Aristotle, along with the earlier Greek natural philosophers, focused more outwardly, on phenomena that could be understood with the senses: the natural world, speech, behavior. Their thinking laid the foundation for modern scientific thought. But even Aristotle's ideas made but a start to the right. Aristotle saw divine action as what began it all—his "unmoved mover"—and invisible causal forces behind motion of every sort.

The strength of truth's two hands became more balanced with culture's perspiration stage (Middle-Axis), but because philosophy tends to take expression from the more inner, reflective side of our rationality (in contrast to politics or economics), medieval philosophical writings tend still to lean toward the archetypally feminine. This continued left-handed emphasis is particularly evident in expressly theistic formulations such as the fourth-century ideas of St. Augustine of Hippo or those of medieval mystics such as Meister Eckhart or Hildegard of Bingen. But the Middle Ages saw also a manifesting of expressly secular philosophy. While St. Thomas Aquinas's ideas were deeply grounded in religious principle, they followed on and extended the tradition of Aristotle. William of Ockham went even further in pressing against the constraints of orthodox religious cosmology.

With the Modern Age (Late-Axis), archetypally masculine philosophical sensibilities moved to the forefront. In the empiricism of Bacon, Locke, and Hume, right-hand truths were assumed to shape the left. Positivist formulations, such those of Saint-Simon and Comte, relied almost exclusively on truth's right hand, as did the more extreme of materialist and early scientific views (Hobbes and Laplace).[4] Dualism became explicit in the seventeenth-century thinking of Descartes[5] (and in a less absolutely cleaved form in the ideas of Leibniz). We see the greatest right-hand preeminence in current times with the claims of extreme behaviorism and scientism that material explanation is all that we need.

Modern Age left-hand cosmologies arose either as a counterbalance to or a reaction against this new right-hand supremacy. The most important include modern forms of idealism (Berkeley, Kant, or Hegel) along with eighteenth- and nineteenth-century romanticism (Rousseau, Schelling, or Goethe). Idealist cosmologies acknowledge the validity of both of truth's hands and assume that they interact, but with them truth's left hand in the end drives the right and determines truth. Spinoza's equating of God with nature set the stage for romanticism's polar response to the growing dominance of right-hand sensibilities.

Note that this progression brings us eventually to the Dilemma of Trajectory, the critical impasse that is central to Creative Systems Theory's argument for Cultural Maturity's further changes. As left-hand sensibilities surrender their dominance to right-hand beliefs, eventually their influence becomes largely eclipsed. Thought's history describes a step-by-step replacing of mysticism by "hard truth." Contemporary thought proclaims final victory for arm's-length objectivity and assumes that future thought will simply reap the rewards of that victory. We are left with the question of whether there is anywhere left to go.

At the least, we are left with the question of whether philosophy has anywhere left to go. If extreme advocates of right-hand truth are correct

---

4 I say "extreme" because most early scientists, and most we associate with the birth of the Scientific Age, were religious people.

5 We might assume that dualism gives equal weight to each hand. However, as I suggested with Chapter Five's image of a sliding third option between polar extremes, which hand predominates is a function of dualism's larger context. The separate-worlds ideas of Descartes, while expressly affirming of religion's place, represented an important victory for distinction over connectedness.

and right-hand truth is all there ever really was (the left hand was just a pleasant illusion), then in effect we've arrived. Philosophy has appropriately reached the end of its usefulness—it is now a historical artifact, its functions replaced by economics, science, and technology. (It is understandable that today we might find so few job openings for philosophers.)

The postmodern current in contemporary thought has at once called for the end of philosophy and vainly attempted to rescue it. Most people who mention philosophers from the last century will describe contributors of existentialist or social constructivist bent. But as I've emphasized, the postmodern contribution can only be a start. While it accurately describes much in current circumstances, it gives us little to help us with the task of proceeding forward.

Realities that confront us as we begin to make our way beyond Transition's precipice help fill out the challenge that philosophy now faces—and also hint at further possibilities. The difficulty faced by the transcendental/left-hand thread in philosophy is most stark. A subjectivity that leaves out the subject—at least in any embodied sense—is ultimately empty. But the empirical/right-hand thread—particularly if we extend it beyond the explicitly philosophical—in the end confronts its own kind of Transitional Absurdity. I've noted how an extreme objectivity that leaves out key parts of the data can hardly be considered objective.

The way in which the concept of Cultural Maturity resolves philosophy's Transitional predicaments should now make basic sense. Cultural Maturity's cognitive reordering does three things with regard to philosophy's left- and right-hand traditions. First, it challenges either hand's claim to be the last word (and just as much views that might split the difference or make opposite views separate but equal). Second, it emphasizes the importance not just of systemically reframing differences between these traditions, but also of finding fresh ways to think about how such differences have taken varying expression depending on when you look (as CST does with Patterning in Time concepts). And finally, it steps back and affirms the possibility of more dynamic and encompassing ways of understanding the contributions of each of these traditions and also of making sense of the larger narrative that together they reflect.

Pattern language concepts that give full expression to human experience's whole-box-of-crayons complexity alter how we understand the whole philosophical endeavor. With Creative Systems Theory's more integrated picture, neither hand gets away unscathed. And at the same time, the truth of each hand becomes more robust, more multihued in conception, and more provocatively part of something larger. While in some small way, we see this result with any sphere of understanding, it manifests in especially striking and consequential ways for the particularly defining systemic relationships that through history have been the concern of philosophy. The diagram in Figure 6-1 provides an outline:

Cultural Stage[6]	Left-hand Preeminence		Right-hand Preeminence
Pre-Axis	Animism		
Early-Axis	Plato, the more spiritual classical Eastern philosophies [the more secular of Eastern philosophies – Taoism, for example – can be thought of as dualistic]		Aristotle, Democritus, Confucious
Middle-Axis	St. Augustine, Meister Eckhard, Hildegard of Bingen		William of Ockham, Thomas Aquinas
Late-Axis	Kant, Schelling, Rousseau, Hegel, Bergson, Teilhard de Chardin		Descartes [or dualism], Newton, Locke, Hume, Compte, and the modern analytic philosophers
Transition	The more extreme of New Age and environmental beliefs	The more extreme of postmodern beliefs	Scientism,[7] extreme behaviorism, the technological gospel
Early Integration	The more mature of religious, Transformational/ New Paradigm, and environmental perspectives	The more mature of postmodern perspectives	The cutting edge of modern science, and the more mature of Post-Industrial/ Information Age perspectives

Fig. 6-1. Philosophy and Patterning in Time

6 When the more "horizontal," left-hand versus right-hand aspect of polarity is most pertinent as it is with philosophy, it helps to turn the Creative Function on its side.

7 While scientism is not limited to Transitional times, it gains wider acceptance with Transitional dynamics (where the archetypally feminine pole is so diminished that it exerts little influence).

Reflecting on this big-picture interpretation, a person could rightly ask whether culturally mature perspective is itself best thought of as philosophy. The postmodern argument for the end of philosophy—at least as a pursuit of final abstracted truths—is legitimate. And culturally mature truth is never just philosophical. It is always as much about politics, science, sociology, religion, or art. But with regard to the question of what makes truth true, its concerns certainly parallel those of philosophical inquiry.

Wherever we end up with our answer, Creative Systems Theory succeeds in bringing fresh life to the philosophical enterprise. We find a result similar to what we encountered for the broad study of history. Culturally mature systemic perspective offers that the kind of inquiry that philosophy represents might become newly vital and substantive. Culturally mature truth is necessarily more humble than the ultimate answers to which classical philosophy aspired. But Creative Systems Theory's vantage at the least makes the "big picture" newly relevant—indeed, essential. And the theory succeeds in providing new appreciation for the wonders (along with the wondrous absurdities) of being human. Its perspective offers a kind of practical applicability that philosophy has rarely been able to achieve. Perhaps a time will come when parents no longer cringe—appropriately—when they hear that their children have chosen philosophy as a college major.

Patterning in Space

Creative Systems Theory describes how human systems pattern creatively not just over time, but also in the here and now. Patterning in Space concepts address diversity within human systems of all scales—domains in a society, departments in a university, professions, functions in a business, roles in a family, personality styles, or parts within ourselves. Biological systems inhabit ecological niches. CST proposes that human systems similarly differentiate into a predictable array of creatively ordered psychological/social niches. Over the years, Patterning in Space distinctions have provided many of Creative Systems Theory's most fascinating insights. They've also offered some of the most rewarding—and fun—interactions with colleagues and students.

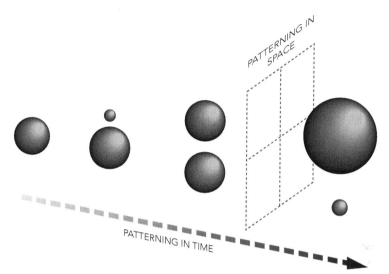

Fig. 6-2. Patterning in Space

Basic Patterning in Space observations have been embedded in previous reflections. The simple observation that human understanding organizes as polar juxtapositions recognizes a basic Patterning in Space relationship (with the additional observation that poles reflect generative complementarities making it a specifically creative kind of relationship). And our box-of-crayons image provides a way to think about here-and-now differences that alerts us both to complementarities and to the role that Integrative Meta-perspective plays in making Patterning in Space distinctions understandable.

While CST Patterning in Space concepts are pertinent any time our interest lies with human here-and-now systemic differences, it is with personality style differences that this aspect of the theory had its beginnings and also where it has been most developed. The Creative Systems Personality Typology presents a nuanced and detailed framework for teasing apart and articulating temperament diversity.

As a psychiatrist, I find it remarkable how different we can be from one another as a function of temperament. Even more remarkable is how we could miss this fact. But these things begin to make sense if we step back sufficiently. Precisely because we live in such different worlds, we can pass by barely seeing one another. And without culturally mature perspective, we may recognize differences but misinterpret them. People who are different then easily become "others;" acknowledged, but known less for who they are than as projections from what we find strange and confusing in ourselves.

As with Patterning in Time's evolutionary notions, attempts to delineate and articulate personality differences tend not to be widely acknowledged and are often simply dismissed.[7] I suspect this is for ultimately related reasons. Again we find a kind of distinction that requires that we draw on the whole of intelligence's multiplicity if it is to be deeply grasped. And we need to get beyond postmodern aversions to judgement and overarching conception. Creative Systems Theory proposes that Cultural Maturity's cognitive changes are needed to deeply appreciate differences of this sort. Without Integrative Meta-perspective, they remain largely invisible to us.

For multiple reasons, in our time sensitivity to temperament differences is coming to have new importance. Most immediately, it helps us deal with conflict in our ever more contentious world. If we look deeply at internal disagreements within groups, for example, often we find that discord has less to do with particular beliefs than with which personality style "reality" will prevail. We find a related kind of conflict between temperament patterns if we look closely at current social/political polarization. I've emphasized how such polarization reflects difference not just in what we think, but how we think. There is value in understanding personality style differences if for no other reason than that such knowledge helps lessen miscommunication and supports people working most effectively together.

One area where people today are beginning to give attention to individual differences is education. Here the focus tends to be on learning styles rather than the deeper kind of difference addressed by the CSPT, but we are better appreciating the fact that different people learn in different ways. And just a bit we are also better recognizing how various students' psychological needs can be very different. Such understanding is key to effective teaching and to the more general creating of environments that are good for kids.

---

7   The one exception is the Myers-Briggs typology (based on the work of Carl Jung) that is often used by people in psychology and business consulting. But the CSPT engages differences with significantly greater depth and with implications that more directly address the tasks of Cultural Maturity.

In the end, better understanding the lenses through which we see our worlds—and how they color experience and need—is essential for self-awareness and self-fulfillment whatever a person's age. And there is a more big-picture reason for understanding temperament diversity that is particularly pertinent to this book's reflections. I've emphasized how the most important questions of our time are systemic questions. A practical way to frame this recognition is that addressing the challenges ahead will require the collaborative input of all the various perspectives that make up the whole of human experience—scientists and artists, liberals and conservatives, thinkers and feelers...and so on.

The Creative Systems Personality Typology provides a way to understand not just the specific strengths and weaknesses of various personality styles, but also how different styles can best work together. It also offers a framework for understanding how personality diversity interplays with other kinds of human difference, such as gender and ethnic diversity. And it provides perspective for making sense of how the experiences of people with different temperaments can differ at various times in developmental processes. It has particular significance for its power as a tool for supporting the kind of creative collaboration on which a healthy future will more and more depend.

The Creative Systems Personality Typology

In first introducing Patterning in Time notions in Chapter Three, I noted that I would go into greater depth in describing them than with most other notions in the book. Given space limitations, our look at the Creative Systems Personality Typology must necessarily be abridged. But because of the significant insights it offers, I will similarly give it somewhat more extended attention.

I've observed that Creative Systems Theory applies the same language when making Patterning in Time and Patterning in Space distinctions. A bare-boned look at how CST approaches temperament differences begins with the recognition that people with different personality styles are most gifted with regard to the various sensibilities that I've associated with different stages in formative process. (They most embody the intelligences and relationships between polar tendencies needed to support those stage-specific creative tasks.) Using CST language, more Early-Axis types have greatest natural affinity with more "inspiration stage" sensibilities, more Middle-Axis types with more "perspiration stage" sensibilities, and more Late-Axis types with more "finishing and polishing" sensibilities.

We can identify the basic contours of Early-, Middle-, and Late-Axis personality differences fairly readily in the goings-on of daily life. (As I will get back to, Pre-Axial personality dynamics represent a special case in modern culture.) For example, within a business, we have the wild creatives and nerdy "eggheads" over in research and development. We also have the managers and workers who take R%D's innovations and get them first into a practical form and then into production. And we have the marketing and financial types who add ideas about what is needed to make the product attractive to its buyers, take care of money matters, and do the selling.

We need to keep a couple of recognitions in mind in order to avoid misunderstanding. First, while for the sake of simplicity we can think in terms of categories—Early, Middle, and Late personality "types"— CSPT categories exist along a continuum. When we say a color is "green," at the same time we know that there are lots of different greens, indeed that there is no absolute line that makes one color blue-green and another greenish blue. In the same sense, with any person's personality we are dealing with balances and interplays—the unique expression of a multifaceted life.

We also need to appreciate how no temperament has an advantage when it comes to development. The most common confusion in getting started with Creative Systems personality concepts is to view "later" personality styles as somehow further along in their growth than "earlier" ones. While Patterning in Time and Patterning in Space concepts use the same language, creative stages and personality styles are separate concerns. Each of us goes through the same sequence of creative realities over the course of our development (and within any endeavor we undertake). At the same time, different people at the same developmental stage have special affinities for the qualities with which a particular stage imbues reality. The latter defines personality style.

The fact of Early-, Middle-, and Late-Axis difference is only the starting point when applying the typology. Within each personality style axis, the theory also distinguishes more Upper and Lower, Outer and Inner "aspects" and personality constellations. We know these differences from everyday experience. Some people live most from their heads or from similarly elevated spiritual aspects of experience, while others are more down to earth. Some people give greatest attention to more in-the-world concerns, while with others, more personal, internal elements in experience have the greater importance.[8]

On the CSPT website (www.CSPThome.org) and in *Creative Systems Theory*, I go into detail with regard to each of the theory's basic temperament patterns. I describe general personality characteristics. I note common strengths and weaknesses. I touch on how each personality style engages and applies different aspects of intelligence's multiplicity. And I examine where each most and least easily relates with other temperaments. I also look at where different personality styles are most likely to miss the mark in their thinking and where each may be particularly vulnerable psychologically. Here I will limit observations to some basic reflections adapted from the book that address general personality characteristics.

Pre-Axial Patterns:

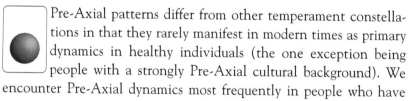

Pre-Axial patterns differ from other temperament constellations in that they rarely manifest in modern times as primary dynamics in healthy individuals (the one exception being people with a strongly Pre-Axial cultural background). We encounter Pre-Axial dynamics most frequently in people who have

---

8 I've noted how the use of terms like "higher consciousness" tend to reflect ideological beliefs. An understanding of temperament helps fill out this observation. We encounter something similar when we equate intelligence with rationality or progress with onward-and-upward technological advancement. In each case, certain Upper Pole patterns can be given an advantage in our judgements. CST makes clear that no temperament has a leg up when it comes to Cultural Maturity. Cultural Maturity is a reflection of Capacitance, and there no temperament has an advantage. In Chapter Four I made reference to a related kind of trap in distinguishing Integrative Meta-perspective from humanistic and spiritual notions that equate identity with some inner essence, core or "true" self. In doing so, they make temperaments in which Inner dynamics predominate more authentic and evolved. With more spiritual ideologies, we can also often find people making the temperament axes where Inner sensibilities reflect the archetypally feminine at is purest most "enlightened."

significant psychological or neurological limitations. Because such dynamics are principally of interest to those in the helping professions, they are beyond the scope of this discussion of normal variation.

Early-Axis Patterns:

 Early-Axis temperaments reflect a special affinity with the inspiration stage in formative process—that period when the buds of new creation first find their way into the world of the manifest. The reality of Early-Axis individuals is born from the organizing sensibilities of possibility and imagination.

Following are a few quotes that capture Early-Axis sensibilities and values: From Albert Einstein, "He who can no longer wonder, no longer feel amazement, is as good as dead." From Miles Davis, "I'll play it first and tell you what it is later." From Henry David Thoreau, "It is life near the bone where it is sweetest." From Orson Welles, "I don't say we all ought to misbehave, but we ought to look as if we could." And from Pablo Picasso, "Everything is miraculous. It is miraculous that one does not melt in one's bath."

Where do we find Earlies? Often they work with young children (a grade school teacher, a day-care worker). Frequently they become artists—visual artists (particularly those of more abstract inclination), dancers (particularly those whose aesthetic tends toward the improvisational), musicians (most jazz musicians, some classical and many rock and roll musicians), or writers (particularly poets and most writers of science fiction). Earlies also make important contributions in the sciences. (Many of science's major innovators have been Earlies—though the larger number of scientists are Lates.) Recently, Earlies have starred in the high-tech revolution. (Steve Jobs, Bill Gates, and Elon Musk are all Earlies.) Most people who teach reflective techniques such as meditation and yoga are Earlies. (It is Earlies who are most attracted to things spiritual, particularly practices with roots in Early-Axis cultural times.)

A few notable Earlies beyond those I've quoted: Leonardo da Vinci, Georgia O'Keeffe, Rainer Maria Rilke, Isadora Duncan, Mary Cassatt, Pablo Neruda, Anaïs Nin, Howard Hughes, John Coltrane, Boris Karloff, Buckminster Fuller, Frank Zappa, Nikola Tesla, Jack Nicholson, and Mrs. Saunders (my kindergarten teacher). More notorious Earlies include Charles Manson, David Kaczynski, and Rasputin.

This listing skews toward the more manifest Early-Axis types. This is in no way to suggest that they have greatest importance. As is the case with every axis, Uppers and Outers are most in the world and thus tend to be most visible. It is only with the more universally manifest world of Late-Axis personality structures that we see Lower/Inner personalities acknowledged historically, and even then they are underrepresented. Mrs. Saunders is the only Early/Lower/Inner in this list.

The Early's defining intelligence is the imaginal, the language of symbol, myth, and metaphor (for the modern Early, as experienced within the rational/material context of today's Late-Axis culture). In keeping with their relationship to the earliest parts of formative process, Earlies tend to have an affinity for the beginnings of things, and of all axes, they are the most comfortable with situations where the unknown outweighs the known. Earlies can take great joy in the nonsensical and contradictory. (From Lewis Carroll in *Through the Looking Glass:* "'Contrariwise,' continued Tweedledee, 'if it was so, it might be; and if it were so, it would be: but as it isn't, it ain't. That's logic.'") The greatest contributions of Earlies often derive from their fascination with underlying principle and pattern. (I am reminded of Albert Einstein's famous assertion, "I am interested in God's thoughts; the rest are details.") And Early/Lowers in particular tend to be more comfortable in their bodies than other temperaments and derive particular fulfillment through bodily experience. (Indeed, for many Earlies, body and spirit can be hard to distinguish.)

With Early/Uppers, qualities such as imaginativeness, intuitiveness, charisma, and spiritual and artistic sensitivity predominate. We often see Early/Upper/Inner sensibilities in poets, painters, and in people drawn to the more ascendant and ascetic of Eastern spiritual practices. Where Early/Upper/Outer aspects are strongest, the Early/Upper's imaginativeness manifests with greatest visibility—through more dramatic forms of artistic expression or through scientific or technical invention. It is here we find the notorious "mad professor."

With Early/Lowers, attributes like connection to nature and mystery, a deep capacity to nurture, and spontaneity are most prominent. With Early/Lower/Inners, this can manifest in environmental work, the teaching of young children, or the more reflective of artistic endeavors. With Early/Lower/Outers we tend to see spontaneity's wilder aspects, as with rock and roll and jazz musicians and dancers who draw on more improvisational aesthetics. Salvador Dali once exclaimed, "I do not take drugs—I am drugs."

Below are some basic qualities and characteristics that we see with the various Early-Axis aspects:

EARLY UPPER INNER
Intuitive, spiritual
Magical child
Essence is important
Meditative disciplines
Eastern philosophy

EARLY UPPER OUTER
Major innovators
Charismatic
Visual artists, poets
Magical relationship with
computers, physical sciences

EARLY LOWER INNER
Ability to nurture
Deep connection to nature
and darkness
Rich inner world
Good with young children

EARLY LOWER OUTER
Spontaneity, improvisation
Playful or "wild" child
Felt closeness to death,
birth, and possibilities
Dancers, musicians,
sculptors

Middle-Axis Patterns:

Middle-Axis temperaments most strongly embody perspiration stage sensibilities, those we find as new creation struggles into crude, but now solid, manifestation. While Earlies identify most with the first improvisational sparks of creation, Middles find greatest meaning turning sparks into usable fire. This requires the ability to provoke and nurture the flames—blow air on them so they will heighten—and, simultaneously, to contain the flames, so that the fire burns usefully and safely. The Middle-Axis fire both does work and warms the hearth of community.

Here are a few words of familiar Middles: From Albert Schweitzer, "A man can only do what he can do. But if he does that each day, he can sleep at night and do it again the next day." From Margaret Mead, "One of the oldest human needs is having someone wonder where you are when you don't come home at night." From Douglas MacArthur, "In war there is no substitute for victory." From Abraham Lincoln, "The better part of a man's life consists of his friendships." From Winston Churchill, "This is a lesson: Never give in—never, never, never, never." From Samuel Johnson, "Great works are performed not by strength, but by perseverance." And from Jesse James, "Everybody loves an outlaw. At least they never forget 'em."

Middles often become teachers, managers in business, military officers, social workers, athletes and coaches, union bosses, ministers or priests, physicians (about an equal balance of Middle/Upper and Late/Upper), politicians (a similar balance), police officers and firefighters, bankers, loggers, owners of family businesses, machinists, miners, and carpenters. In addition, Middles make up the greater portion of stay-at-home parents. (It is with Middle-Axis that we find the strongest identification with home, family, and community.) Women who think of themselves first as wives and mothers are commonly Middles, as are the most devoted husbands and fathers. Middle-Axis individuals of both sexes frequently play strong roles in their neighborhoods and churches, and in social service organizations. Most of the "real work" in society is done by Middles.

Some better-known Middles beyond those cited include Teddy Roosevelt, Mother Teresa, Margaret Thatcher, Joe Louis, Billy Graham, Babe Ruth, Florence Nightingale, Colin Powell, Aretha Franklin, Julia Child, Queen Victoria, Johnny Cash, J. Edgar Hoover, Cesar Chavez, and Betty Friedan. More notorious Middles include Joseph Stalin, Adolf Hitler, Ma Barker, and, as above, Jesse James. Again, Lower Pole figures—particularly Lower/Inners—are not well represented in this list. But Middle/Lower is where we find many of the most important, if unheralded, figures in our lives: the neighborhood police officer or firefighter, the friend who is there no matter what, the parent who puts a special note in a child's lunchbox.

Emotional-moral intelligence, the intelligence of heart and guts (as it manifests within Late-Axis culture) orders the Middle's world. The stuff of the heart holds sway in Middle/Inner and Middle/Lower temperaments—where the archetypally feminine is strongest. Harder sensibilities—the stuff of guts and fortitude—dominate with Middle/Upper and Middle/Outer temperaments. In each case, Middle-Axis dynamics move us firmly into the human dimension. Early-Axis and Late-Axis realities are each in their own ways abstracted from the personal. Early-Axis deals with the pre-personal reality of creative buddings; Late-Axis deals with the post-personal world of the intellectual, the social, and the material. Middle-Axis puts us right in the middle, engaged directly in the tasks of mortal existence.

With Middle-Axis personality styles, as with Middle-Axis dynamics more generally, we find polar opposites juxtaposed in near equal balance. Like two ends of a teeter-totter, they simultaneously battle and collude. In the Middle-Axis psyche, strength struggles with weakness, thoughts with feelings, good with evil, domination with submission, control with abandon, honor with dishonor. Meaning for a Middle is a reflection of timely balance (though often of a conflicted sort) between such isometrically interplaying forces. The reward for this creative push-pull is the realization of substance and the satisfaction of a job well done.

Words we might associate with Middle/Upper personalities include fortitude, courage, uprightness, fairness, and moral conviction. Middle/Uppers are often strong leaders. With Middle/Upper/Outers this is frequently formal organizational leadership—the leadership of politicians, captains of industry, coaches, military officers. Middle/Upper/Inner leadership tends to manifest in ways that are more personal and interactional. Upper/Inner sensibilities are common in teachers, managers, and religious leaders. Middle/Upper/Inner leadership commonly has a strong moral component.

People of Middle/Lower temperament tend to be most known for their perseverance, loyalty, capacity to support in relationship, and sometimes for their irreverent sense of humor. For Middle/Lower/Inners, the most defining relationships tend to be with friends, family, and immediate community. Besides being good parents, Middle/Lower/Inners often contribute through working as teachers (particularly with children and adolescents), as social workers, in nursing, or in the food industry. For Middle/Lower/Outers, the key relationships tend to be with community in a broader sense, with team members, or even more broadly, with one's ethnic group or nation. Middle/Lower/Outers become farmers, soldiers, police officers, carpenters, and professional athletes. It is they who do the hands-on protecting and heavy lifting of society.

Below are some basic qualities and characteristics that we see with the various Middle-Axis aspects:

MIDDLE UPPER INNER
Committed to learning
and community
Strong moral values
Inner emotional control
Priests, teachers

MIDDLE UPPER OUTER
Good managers of people
and organizations
Understands control dynamics
Political savvy
Committed "doers"

MIDDLE LOWER INNER
Interpersonal committment
Value hearth, home and
community
Unpretentious but hard-
working
Caring, supportive parents

MIDDLE LOWER OUTER
Strength and endurance in
the workplace
Get things done
Strong sense of loyalty and
comradeship
Police, firefighters,
construction workers and
soldiers

Late-Axis Patterns:

Late-Axis patterns correspond to the finishing and polishing stage in formative process—the developmental period that turns our attention to questions of detail and completion. Rational/material intelligence orders experience, bringing emphasis to the intellect and to the more refined (manifest) aspects of the emotional and the aesthetic. Because Late-Axis is the most natively outer of patterns, Lates tend to function most easily and efficiently in the external world.

Following are a few words of well-known Lates: From John F. Kennedy, "In times of turbulence and change, it is more true than ever that knowledge is power." From Elizabeth Cady Stanton, "In a word, I am always busy, which is perhaps the chief reason I am always well." From Alfred, Lord Tennyson, "'Tis better to have loved and lost, than never to have loved at all." From Francis Bacon, "Reading maketh a full man, conference a ready man, and writing an exact man." From Alexander Dumas, "Nothing succeeds like success." From Bill Blass, "When in doubt, wear red." From T.H. Huxley, "Science is nothing but trained and organized common sense." From Sophie Tucker, "I have seen poor and I have seen rich. Rich is better." And from Bertrand Russell, "To be able to fill leisure intelligently is the last product of civilization."

Lates often become professors, writers, lawyers, CEOs, scientists, fashion models, ballet or modern dancers, Wall Street financiers, marketers, or actors. More frequently than with people from other axes,

Martin Luther King, Jr.; Mother Teresa: Manfredo Ferrari, Wikimedia; Margaret Thatcher: Marion S. Trikosko, Wikimedia; Babe Ruth various individuals can differ widely in their inclinations.[9] Within Late-Axis we find the people who are most rational in their perspective, and also those who tend most toward the romantic. We find the people who are most materialistically driven, and at once many of those most committed to artistic and intellectual pursuits where monetary remuneration can be slight. We find the people most aggressively in the world, and also many of those most internal and reflective in their proclivities.

Some familiar Lates beyond those cited include: Walter Cronkite, Marie Curie, Carl Sagan, Julia Roberts, Sammy Davis, Jr., Elizabeth Taylor, Frank Sinatra, Mikhail Gorbachev (really more Middle than Late, but notable because he embodies significantly more Late than any previous Soviet leader), Gloria Steinem, Woodrow Wilson, Johnny Carson, Clark Gable, Mikhail Baryshnikov, William F. Buckley, and Robert Redford. Less savory sorts tend to engage in white collar crime, so are less visible and less often prosecuted than Early and Late lawbreakers—Michael Milken comes to mind, along with those involved in the Enron debacle and the investment bank excesses of the 2008 financial collapse.

When we say someone is scholarly or intellectual, most often we are making reference to a Late. And more than other temperaments, Lates tend to be materially successful. They are the most natively competitive and the most likely to value external reward. Lates can be quite creative, but their creativity tends to be of a different sort than the whole-cloth originality of Earlies. Late-Axis scientists are more likely to be recognized for the precision and detail of their experimental work and for their ability to bring together existing work to reach new conclusions. Late-Axis visual artists, dancers, and musicians tend to work from established traditions or written scores and make their primary creative contributions through refinement and subtlety of aesthetic expression.

Lates tend to value and manifest social skills. This can take highly formal expression—etiquette and the fine art of diplomacy come naturally to many Lates. As often, it manifests in a simple ease and comfort

---

9 A look to the Creative Function provides explanation. It is here that we see the greatest natural separation between poles.

in the social sphere. When we say someone has "personality" or "style," when we say someone is sophisticated or looks "sharp," we are usually referring to a Late. More than other temperaments, Lates attend to physical appearance, and generally pull off looking good. Estee Lauder offered this advice: "Never just 'run out for a few minutes' without looking your best. This is not vanity—it is self-liking."

The qualities that most stand out with Late/Upper personalities are clarity of thought, verbal facility, and the ability to deal easily and effectively with the material world. With Late/Upper/Inners, the more intellectual of these qualities stand out. University professors, scientific researchers, and nonfiction writers commonly have Late/Upper/Inner personalities. Late/Upper/Inner is also where we find the greatest appreciation for the formal. With Late/Upper/Outers, more external and material concerns take center stage. Here we commonly find the people who are most facile with money and the complexities of the business world—corporate executives, economists, media moguls, and stockbrokers. We also find "serious" media personalities such as television commentators. While for Late/Upper/Inners the intellect resides most comfortably in the ivory tower, Late/Upper/Outers apply it to more worldly concerns.

With Late/Lower patterns, qualities such as social ease, talent, sensuality, and emotional presence often most stand out. Of all personality groups, Late/Lowers are most likely to enjoy being "on stage." Late/Lowers often have a rich sense of the dramatic, as well as the smoothness and presence needed to pull it off. People in the performing arts tend to have at least some Late/Lower in their makeup, as do the great majority of fashion models and television entertainers. Where the balance is toward Inner, the dramatic focus highlights emotional and aesthetic nuance. Late/Lower/Inner is a common personality style of dancers and actors. Novelists and visual artists of a more realist bent also often find their creative source in Late/Lower/Inner sensibilities, as do interior and fashion designers. With Late/Lower/Outers we find the people with the greatest capacity to project and be visible. Late/Lower/Outers tend to be particularly successful at marketing and promotion (both of things and of themselves). They define the entertainment industry—glamour and celebrity are Late/Lower/Outer words. The more glittery and flamboyant of actors and actresses tend to have Late/Lower/Outer personalities, as do the more promoted of popular musicians. More day-to-day, Late/Lower/Outers may work for advertising agencies or sell high-end clothing or real estate.

Below are some basic qualities and characteristics that we see with the various Late-Axis aspects:

LATE UPPER INNER
Philosophical/intellectual
Good synthesizers
Good delineation and
understanding of detail
Values objectivity

LATE UPPER OUTER
Values directness, clarity and
succinctness
Sophisticated and worldly
Tends to be good with money
Effective corporate leaders

LATE LOWER INNER
Aesthetic sensitivity
Grace and refinement
Emotional attentiveness
Artistic expressiveness

LATE LOWER OUTER
Ability to project oneself —
to be "on stage"
Emotionally articulate
Strong personal presence,
sense of the dramatic
Performers, media,
marketing

Temperament and the Tasks of Cultural Maturity

Any approach to understanding human differences can assist us in learning to better understand ourselves and get along with others, but the Creative Systems Personality Typology does so in ways not found with other approaches. Of particular importance, while the typology describes the specifics of differences with particular detail, in addition it addresses mechanisms, helps us understand just why it is that we see the differences that we do. In the process, it also helps us better appreciate how such differences may contribute both to understanding what ultimately makes something true and to addressing what Cultural Maturity's changes ask of us.

One way the CSPT has direct pertinence to the tasks of Cultural Maturity concerns the importance of separating the wheat from the chaff in our thinking. I've observed that we can predict the kind of ideological traps a person will be most vulnerable to by teasing apart psychological structures and patterns. The typology describes how we can make a solid guess if we have information about temperament axis, aspects, and also Capacitance. This is the case both with regard to the

Barbara Walters: John Matthew Smith, Wikimedia; Dorothy Hamill, Wikimedia; John Matthew Smith, Wikimedia; Sammy Davis, Jr.: Hugo van Gelderen/Anefo, Wikimedia kinds of social/political ideologies a person is most likely to ascribe to and common broader kinds of ideological affiliations (religious/philosophical/scientific).

Reflections from my years leading yearlong trainings at the Institute provide concrete illustration of where the CSPT's contribution to Cultural Maturity may be most ultimately significant. I would select participants for programs according to a couple of criteria. Capacitance is one— people needed to be "up to the task." But just as important, ultimately, was personality style. I chose participants so that temperament diversity was fully represented. Each "crayon" in the creative box thus had its advocates—and advocates of a formidable sort. One of the things that most struck people on the first day of the yearlong training was how different many of the people in the room were from the people they were most used to spending time with. And because of the universally high Capacitance, these differences could not just be dismissed.

Most immediately, having that diversity—and that particular kind of diversity—in the room was powerful at a personal level. One may never be a jazz musician, a professional football player, or an advertising executive, but if one can begin to understand what might make such people who they are—and better, even slightly embody their felt realities—these people's presence can help one more deeply engage creation's full systemic complexity in oneself. Partway through the year, I would engage the group in a deep immersion into the Creative Systems Personality Typology to help make these learnings more conscious.

Having that particular kind of diversity in the room also became essential for our shared work together. The mosaic of realities that personality style differences represent supported the collaborative efforts needed to address the deeply systemic questions these emerging culturally mature leaders were there to engage. Near the end of the training, I'd have participants divide up into small think tank teams to work on future issues in specific domains—education, government, business, and so on. By that time, they had come to recognize that choosing like-minded team members was not the right approach if they wanted culturally mature results. If participants' teams were going to be most powerfully creative, they would need the contributions of each basic temperament axis.

At the end of the year, I would ask people which of all the various approaches we had made use of in the training had most helped them understand the concept of Cultural Maturity and embody needed changes. For a great many, the need to consciously grapple with the fact of temperament differences had had the greatest effect. Having this living complexity immediately present in the room made each session an exercise in holding the larger whole of what it means to be human, and more specifically, how we need to be human in our time.

The CSPT and Diversity More Generally

I've noted that a creative framing of temperament differences can help us by offering perspective with regard to other kinds of diversity such as gender diversity and race. This kind of observation will necessarily be controversial in today's social climate. But it can help us get beyond the easy (and often polarizing) assumptions of identity politics and bring greater nuance to our thinking.

In Chapter Four, I made beginning reference to the basis of how this applies to gender in describing that normative 60/40 balance of archetypal qualities. Each temperament axis includes equal numbers of men and women. But within each axis we find a somewhat greater percentage of women inhabiting the Inner and Lower (more archetypally feminine) aspects and a somewhat greater percentage of men inhabiting Outer and Upper (more archetypally masculine) aspects.

Observations that relate to race and ethnicity are likely to be even more controversial, but in a similar way they can help us to get beyond both bigotries and fears of acknowledging difference. People of various ethnic backgrounds differ not just by virtue of cultural experience, but also with regard to the balance of various personality style patterns within their populations. For example, in the United States we see a somewhat higher percentage than average of Early/Lower and Middle/Lower personalities in Native American, South Sea Islander, Hispanic, and African American populations; a somewhat higher percentage than average of Early/Upper/Inner and Middle/Upper/Inner personalities in Americans of Asian background; a somewhat higher percentage than average of Middle-Axis personalities (both upper and lower) in Americans of Middle Eastern, Eastern European, Scandinavian, and Irish extraction; and a somewhat higher percentage than average of Late-Axis personalities in Americans of predominantly English or Western European heritage.[10]

The differences here are in most cases small, but they can have significant consequences. For example, traditional public education does very poorly at addressing the needs of Early/Lower and Middle/Lower kids—whatever their background. (I know firsthand. As with most sculptors, I have a lot of Early/Lower in my personality.) The aspects of intelligence where these personality styles on average most excel are largely ignored. Not surprisingly, youth from cultural groups where these personalities styles manifest with higher than average frequency can feel estranged in public education and thrive there less well than one might hope and expect. This observation suggests that while increasing the amount of educational content that directly addresses cultural backgrounds has an important place in educational reform, making education more responsive to our multiple intelligences and to the unique realities of different personality temperaments may be as much or more important in the long run.

---

10 Again, these are normative observations. Many of the most visible people of African American heritage, for example, are Lates—Barack and Michelle Obama, Sidney Poitier, Billie Holiday, Sammy Davis, Jr.

CHAPTER SEVEN

Confronting Ultimate Human Questions

A particularly provocative consequence of Creative Systems Theory's radical newness is the way it lets us address questions that in times past have either left us baffled or produced at best limited answers. Such questions can relate to quite ultimate topics, eternal concerns that we might easily think are beyond the province of mere mortals. Cultural Maturity's cognitive changes help us make such questions more understandable. And Creative Systems Theory patterning concepts often provide quite specific answers.

We've already made a solid beginning with how this might be so. Chapter Two's look at the evolution of narrative challenged us to rethink what the human story is ultimately about. Chapter Three, in bringing fresh attention to the workings of change in human systems, helped clarify the role of polarity in how we think and provided essential insight into just how understanding works. Chapter Four, in examining the Myth of the Individual, challenged us to fundamentally rethink both human identity and what makes human interactions relationships. Chapter Five engaged the creative underpinnings of human intelligence and its role in our experience of purpose. And Chapter Six's examination of philosophy's history, in addressing how belief has changed over time, brought us closer to answering just how it is that we have come to think of certain things as true.

In a general sense, we can think of both Creative Systems Theory's application of a creative frame and the more specific concept of Cultural Maturity in this way: CST's new Fundamental Organizing Concept addresses the ultimate question of what in the end most makes us human. And while the particular demands of our time are not so much foundational concerns, the fact that Cultural Maturity's "growing up" as a species makes those demands understandable—and in the process more addressable—gives the concept an ultimate kind of importance.

This chapter includes short pieces that apply a creative frame to a handful of particularly ultimate topics. The first piece takes on the debate between free will and determinism. The second pushes beyond the historically conflicting worldviews of science and religion. And the last turns to a couple of related, particularly ultimate ultimate questions: How do we best understand existence as a whole—the whole shebang—and how do we best make sense of our place in it?

The fact that Creative Systems Theory is able to help us with such quandaries is a direct consequence of the leap in understanding that Integrative Meta-perspective makes possible. It turns out that even just asking any of the questions we will look at in ways that can produce ultimately useful answers requires systemic understanding of the more dynamic and complete sort that becomes possible with Cultural Maturity's cognitive reordering. The parental truths of times past can't help us with such questions, and dualistic notions of any sort necessarily leave us short. And we can't get there if we make only certain intelligences the definers of truth. Creative Systems Theory's application of a creative frame takes us the additional step of letting us be more specific and detailed in our answers. It also helps answers come alive. Just how it does further affirms the power and newness of CST's approach.

These three short pieces are adapted from more extended reflections included in the book *Creative Systems Theory*.

Free Will and Determinism

The free-will-versus-determinism debate fundamentally challenges usual understanding. You would not be reading this book, and I would not have written it, if we did not believe in free will in some form. Yet basic cause and effect, at least as classical science conceives of it, describes a deterministic world. Free will and determinism each seem self-evident, but limited to the assumptions of Modern Age thought they imply mutually exclusive realities.

The needed new picture follows from how Integrative Meta-perspective alters how we think about conscious awareness and how a creative frame changes our experience of determination. I began my extended piece in *Creative Systems Theory* on this topic by describing a television series in which physicist Stephen Hawking makes the standard classical science argument that free will is an illusion.

I propose that while this conclusion follows logically from accepted assumptions, it really doesn't hold up to scrutiny. And I describe how familiar beliefs about free will just as much fail the test of considered reflection—at least reflection when made from the vantage of Integrative Meta-perspective.

The simple fact that the free-will-versus-determinism debate takes the form of a polarity at least suggests that a more systemic picture should be possible. And the fact that we can understand positions in terms of polarity's underlying symmetry and the kinds of intelligence that polar advocacies most draw on further supports this conclusion. Humanist and spiritual sorts are likely to emphasize freedom of will, while more scientific and behavioral types are apt to emphasize deterministic conclusions and give will diminished significance or dismiss it outright.

For these brief reflections, I will draw on a more specific polarity-related observation. A simple way to think about the free-will-versus-determinism debate and how it might be reconciled turns to the recognition that Modern Age beliefs about both will and determination have been directly tied to how we have viewed the relationship between mind and body. In modern times we've conceived of mind and body as separate. We've also seen each functioning according to basic rules of cause and effect. In this world, awareness is "captain of the cellular ship"—free and unfettered. And the body, as anatomy and physiology, functions according to basic engineering principles. Free will and determinism each have their own separate, rationally understandable realities.

Cultural Maturity's cognitive changes reveal a picture that is more of a whole, more expressly systemic. It is also a picture in which mind and body each come to function according to more dynamic principles. With Integrative Meta-perspective we come to appreciate that while awareness helps facilitate possibility, by itself it doesn't determine it. And we leave behind thinking of the life of the body only in mechanistic terms. We find a more expressly creative reality all the way around, one that fundamentally alters the free-will-versus-determinism debate.

The fact that a larger reality might exist is more a part of our daily experience than we might imagine. Certainly this is true for conscious awareness. Few truths become more obvious when practicing the craft of the psychotherapist, for example, than how different the reality of conscious awareness[1] is from how the conscious mind tends to view itself. (Comic Emo Philips once quipped: "I used to think the brain was the most important organ in the body, until I realized who was telling me that.") The fact that conscious awareness is limited in what it can grasp is exactly as it should be. Much of our functioning works best without volition's interference. (Recall Kipling's centipede who walks gracefully with its hundred legs until praised for her exquisite memory.)

I think of my own experience as a writer. In an earlier footnote I observed that some of my best insights wake me up in the middle of the night. I also get a lot of my best ideas when on road trips, while driving through a mountain pass, or along the ocean. Insights often come unbidden. Sometimes they relate to topics that I had not before even considered. Certainly, they are not products of "will" as we conventionally think of it. And such experiences reveal conscious awareness to be a rather fleeting basis for identity. At the least, awareness comes and goes with sleeping and waking. But at various times, it can also often provide very different views of reality.

In a similar way, a more systemic kind of understanding is coming to permeate the best of thinking about the body. As we learn more deeply

---

1   The quandary I address here is often spoken of as part of the "consciousness problem." In Chapter Three, I noted that because the word "consciousness" gets applied in multiple ways with wholly different implications, I try to avoid it. To add to the confusion, each way tends to leave us short. The term can be used to describe what here I am calling "conscious awareness" (reflective awareness—being aware of being aware). Consciousness in this sense is frequently confused with identity as a whole (as with "captain of the cellular ship" assumptions). The term can also be used to refer to our more general ability to experience. It then often becomes one half of a duality—subjective versus objective. Or in more extreme interpretations that make inner experience the locus of truth, consciousness can become but another word for spirit (and the term's use a giveaway for Unity Fallacy thinking). We also confront how cognitive science's tendency to reduce understanding to a mechanistic worldview can have it dismiss much that is most important in awareness's contribution. Here I will speak of conscious awareness and avoid the term "consciousness." And I will be referring to conscious awareness in a way that gets beyond the traps both of identification and dismissal—as an essential ingredient in human intelligence's dynamic workings.

about the complex workings of the endocrine system, for example, or about connections that exist between the gut and cognitive functioning, we find not a mechanical body, but a living body. And as I've described, when we look more psychologically, we find a body that is in important ways intelligent.

A simple thought experiment helps make the result when we think more systemically about the body more concrete. Imagine a gifted running back in football making his way down the field, rapidly cutting this way and that. The running back's cuts take place more quickly, and in ways that are more nuanced, than could ever happen by consciously choosing them one at a time. The conscious aspects of intelligence simply aren't built to function that rapidly or complexly. Does this mean, then, that the running back is not choosing? And, more specifically, does it then mean that, because his body moves before he "chooses," what we witness is nothing more than mechanical reflex following the rules of a deterministic world? Such interpretations leave us with a less than convincing picture. At the least they leave us with bothersome questions. Are the outcomes of games then predetermined—or, alternatively, perhaps random? Either way, we are left wondering why we would attend a football game—and perhaps feeling a bit duped. I think the problem lies with the fact that our explanations really don't hold up. Clearly in the running back's movements we witness something that is not just vital, but intelligent, and profoundly so.

Integrative Meta-perspective provides a more conceptually demanding—but also ultimately simpler—interpretation when it comes to both conscious awareness and the life of the body. In the process, it also fundamentally alters how we understand both human will and the dynamics of determination.

With the recognition that the greater portion of our psychological functioning happens well outside of awareness, conscious awareness— and with it will—comes to have a new, at once more humble, and ultimately profound, role. Rather than willfully determining our actions, it serves as a facilitator and catalyst for intelligence's richly creative workings. Integrative Meta-perspective reveals that while thinking of free will as free and willful in the unfettered sense implied by our Modern Age may once have benefitted us, today it gets in the way of fully appreciating choice's ultimately more powerful and creative contribution.

With regard to the body, Integrative Meta-perspective in a similar way offers a more interesting and ultimately powerful picture. We come to see the body not as a separate deterministic machine, but as an integral part of who we are as living—and specifically human—beings. A creative frame makes this result more explicit. We recognize how body sensibilities represent a critical, multilayered aspect of intelligence's larger workings. We also better appreciate the rich complexities of its contribution in those workings.

Creative Systems Theory proposes that the Modern Age free-will-versus-determinism debate has been a product of a developmentally appropriate, but systemically incomplete view of the world. It has been based on a falsely framed dichotomy, a juxtaposing of alternative determinisms that together have served to protect us—as polar explanations of every sort do—from life's ultimately rich, but also easily overwhelming uncertainties and complexities.

Integrative Meta-perspective reveals that free will is not so free—nor as much ours to direct—as those of an individualistic bent might prefer. And neither is determination as predetermined as advocates of either a more scientific determinism or the determinisms of religious faith might wish. The more systemic picture that results makes outcomes less readily anticipated, but the particular way that it does also makes outcomes ultimately more significant. While we lose the order of one thing guaranteeing another, we get in exchange the more generative sort of order that makes existence vital. We get creative possibility, and as humans, the particular kind of creative possibility that makes us who we are.

Science and Religion—Toward a Larger Picture
(and How Creative Systems Theory Gets Us Very Close)

The conflicting views of science and religion present a particularly intriguing and consequential "ultimate question" example. Most crudely it asks, Which interpretation is right? The better question might be, How do science and religion relate to one another—if they do at all?

In modern times, we've tended to place the material and the spiritual in wholly separate worlds. This is not an entirely unhelpful solution. It has shielded us from perceived contradictions so basic that they have resulted historically in people being burned at the stake. But this is not a solution that can satisfy for long. Creative Systems Theory describes how, when we step back sufficiently, not only do the material and spiritual relate as aspects of something larger, the specific way they relate reflects dynamics at the heart of what makes us human. It also proposes that in spite of how often through history the relationship between scientific and spiritual belief has appeared adversarial, science and religion have all along been engaged in an essential kind of conspiracy.

With Chapter Five's introduction to Parts Work, I noted an easily startling recognition that commonly confronts people who wish to engage issues that relate specifically to religion or science. In doing Parts Work, neither sort of truth appropriately occupies the Whole-Person/Whole-System leadership chair. It turns out that while the aspects of ourselves that advocate for more spiritual and material sensibilities each have much to add to the Whole-Person/Whole-System chair's reflections, at their best they function as consultants. Within our systemic complexity, religious belief and scientific belief each represent parts.

Creative Systems Theory proposes that our ideas about science and religion at any point in time—as with our ideas about most anything at a point in time—are as much products of how we understand as what is "out there" to understand. And it clarifies how science and religion are less conflicting truths than "ways of knowing," each of which through history has made essential contributions. We come back to the question of narrative and how our answers to it have evolved over time. Science and religion through history become alternative ways of describing a larger story, a story that asks more of us to deeply grasp, but that is also more complete in being more fully reflective of understanding's—and life's—rich vitality and complexity.

Science, Religion, and the Structures of Human Cognition

A basic polarity-related observation emphasized earlier provides a way in. I've described how a single more fundamental polarity underlies any particular polar juxtaposition: difference/multiplicity on one hand and connectedness/oneness on the other. The related observation that polarity, whenever and wherever we find it, juxtaposes more right-hand, archetypally masculine characteristics with qualities of a more left-hand, archetypally feminine adds flesh to this bare-boned picture. Framed creatively, science and religion are expressions of what we see when we view existence as a whole through the lenses of these contrasting/complementary aspects of cognition's creative workings. Science is about collective right-hand, archetypally masculine experience—the "difference/multiplicity" half of ultimate polarity—in its purest manifestation. Religion is about collective left-hand, archetypally feminine sensibility—ultimate polarity's complementary "connectedness/oneness" dimension—similarly cleansed of contamination by the right.

A closer look at the contrasting contributions of science and religion supports this interpretation. Science is about distinction—this as opposed to that. Biology delineates the creaturely into taxonomies of genus and species, chemistry gives us the periodic table and the interplay of atoms and molecules, and classical physics describes objects of differing mass and the this-versus-that laws of material cause and effect. Spiritual/religious experience in contrast highlights oneness. We can think of religious belief through history in terms of four connectedness-related themes: how things arose from the undivided ("in the beginning"), community (congregation and communion), right thought and behavior (shared moral assumptions), and how experiences interrelate (and, in the end, how it all interrelates). In Latin, *re-ligare*, the root of the word "religion," means "to connect." William James put it this way: "In mystic states we both become one with the Absolute and we become aware of our oneness." Integrative Meta-perspective offers that we might see a larger picture. It also offers that we might entertain more dynamic and complete understandings of both science and religion.

The way that Cultural Maturity's cognitive reordering expands our understanding of intelligence adds further substance and nuance to this creative picture. I've described how Modern Age belief not only placed polarities in separate worlds, it also put aspects of intelligence in separate categories. Rationality came to stand distinct, idealized as the basis of final, "objective" understanding, with intelligence's remaining sensibilities then lumped together in a secondary world of "subjective" experience. I've observed that this cleaving of perception served the essential purpose of taking us beyond the strangling constraints of medieval mysticism. But I've also emphasized how the essential challenges ahead for the species demand something more. To be not just intelligent but wise in the sense needed going forward requires the ability to draw consciously, and in a newly possible more integrated fashion, on the whole of our cognitive complexity.

We would expect this more complete picture of intelligence to alter the conclusions of both science and religion. Historically, the most creatively manifest aspect of intelligence—the rational—has given us the more material and mechanistic sensibilities that inform the world of science. Science is not just rational in some "coldly objective" sense. Every good scientist appreciates the "spirit of science" and the awe and wonder of the world it reveals. But at least within classical science, the world is assumed to be rationally understandable. Spiritual/religious experience, in contrast, draws on the more creatively germinal aspects of intelligence. Depending on the stage in culture, that can be animistic/body-focused sensibilities (as with tribal times), the more magical/intuitive sensitivities of the imaginal and mythic (as with the rise of polytheism), or emotional intelligence (as with the moral ardencies of monotheism as we saw in the European Middle Ages). I've touched on how Creative Systems Theory brings detail to how we can understand specific beliefs in terms of the various ways intelligence's generative sensibilities manifest in different times and places. Integrative Meta-perspective, in offering that we might more consciously engage the whole of intelligence's generative multiplicity, reveals the possibility of a more encompassing, and ultimately creative picture for science and religion.

The theory's observation that human developmental processes organize creatively lets us be even more specific. We can use it to map the stories of science and religion over time. We witness this creatively ordered progression in science's evolution from the nature-centered beliefs of tribal times, to more magically dualistic formulations such as that of Aristotle, to views in the Middle Ages that postulated mystically infused forces (as with alchemy), to the scientific method and its formalization with Modern Age understanding. Similarly we see it with religion's evolution from animism, to polytheism, to absolutist monotheism, to the more liberal monotheism of the Reformation.[2]

---

2 This evolution of religious forms refers to the West. I've noted how the more reflective sensibilities of the East have often resulted in stages mani-

Besides helping us make sense of how (and why) the particular beliefs of science and religion have evolved as they have, Creative Systems Theory's developmental formulations also help us understand how the relationship between material and spiritual inclinations has evolved over time. Here two further themes become pertinent. The first concerns which "creative hand" at a particular time has the most prominent influence. I've described how a consistent trend runs through history's evolutionary story. Culture's creative narrative has progressed from a time of archetypally feminine dominance in our tribal beginnings toward today, when archetypally masculine proclivities hold the much larger sway. As we would predict from this progression, we see a parallel evolution over time from realities defined almost wholly in spiritual terms with animistic beliefs toward what we find in our time, a world in which many people hold strong religious beliefs, but in which more material values (scientific, but even more than this, economic) ultimately have greater influence.

The second theme concerns the different ways that the relationship between science's more archetypally masculine and religion's more archetypally feminine worlds have been experienced. The sequence of juxtapositions we discover is just what we would predict if the relationship between science and religion is ultimately creative. In early societies, material and spiritual sensibilities tended to be spoken of almost as one. Later, as with much of the European Middle Ages, material and spiritual inclinations more often took expression in ways that were explicitly at odds. Later still, as with Cartesian dualism, science and religion more comfortably coexisted, but accomplished the feat by, in effect, ignoring each other's presence.

Integrative Meta-perspective suggests the possibility of a more dynamic and encompassing picture of science and religion through history, one in which science and religion, however irreconcilable their

---

festing in ways that can feel more philosophical or even psychological. I place the nature-centered contemplations of Taoism early on in this progression, and the more mythic beliefs of Hinduism and Buddhism's more specifically meditative worldview somewhat later. Beliefs emphasizing strong social authority, such as Confucianism, happened developmentally in parallel with early monotheism in the West. More modern sensibilities have only come with the last century in the East.

conclusions have often seemed, are viewed as having worked together to support and drive culture's creative manifestation.

The Future and Cultural Maturity's Challenge to Science and Religion

Cultural Maturity's cognitive reordering also offers that we might begin to address what may lie ahead. The new picture it suggests holds surprises. For example, we could assume that it would have us stop thinking of science and religion as separate. In one sense that is true, but as I've touched on more generally with our look at polar fallacies, what we find is very different from either some simple merging together or compromise. We could use either the example of Parts Work or the box-of-crayons image I've drawn on throughout the book to clarify this important distinction. If merging together were the task, some oneness-identified part would prevail. If compromise were the task, we would see a parts-talking-to-parts dynamic and a resolution of opposing hues that gives us only muddy brown. With Integrative Meta-perspective, our understandings of science and religion, besides becoming more of a whole, each also become more specific and distinct.[3]

There is also how new formulations in science and religion each themselves become newly systemic, in the sense of at least acknowl-edging the validity of both more left-hand and more right-hand as-pects of understanding. With Cultural Maturity's cognitive reordering, both science and religion manifest in ways that are more dynamic and embracing than what we have known before. This will be necessary

---

3 The Parts Work example adds further nuance. The most immediate con-clusion when doing Parts Work is that neither religion nor science gets to sit in the Whole-Person/Whole-System leadership chair. But Parts Work's third cardinal rule also makes it clear that "crosstalk" between the religion and science chairs similarly leaves us short. This recognition highlights larger historical implications. I've described how such internal debate had a function in times past. We can understand each of history's previous views of how the spiritual and the material relate in terms of it. Such direct con-versation between parts gave us the easy complementarities of more magi-cal thought (as with yin and yang in classical Chinese belief), the warring absolutes of medieval dogmatisms, and the separated-worlds assumptions of Cartesian dualism. Creative Systems Theory argues that it only makes us less going forward.

if science and religion in times ahead are each to fully reflect human understanding. It will also be necessary if science and religion are to effectively contribute to the maturity of perspective that will be essential if, as a species, we are to make wise decisions going forward.

This more fully systemic picture fundamentally challenges traditional assumptions of both science and religion. With regard to science, right off it challenges the common conclusion that science can explain anything if pursued far enough. Cultural Maturity brings the notion that science's method works for everything immediately into question. Seen from a culturally mature perspective, science becomes a kind of tool that is great for some tasks and of limited help for others. We need only think about how little scientific observation as we have known it can tell us about many of the most important things in our lives—love, meaning, creativity, and much more (including, ultimately, the fact of life itself)—to recognize inherent limits to the approach. Integrative Meta-perspective reveals modern science's assumptions that everything is rationally intelligible to be a "faith claim," and in the end a faith claim that does not hold up. We best answer science's Question of Referent by observing that science's method is appropriate for those aspects of reality that are in fact materially measurable and rationally intelligible. Put another way, science is great in most instances for teasing apart the difference/multiplicity aspects of experience. For this, we rightly celebrate its considerable power.

Cultural Maturity's cognitive reordering also confronts classical science by bringing into question its mechanistic and objectivist foundations. Integrative Meta-perspective makes clear that not only does mechanistic thinking fail when it comes to explaining everything, in the end it also confronts limits when it comes to the difference/multiplicity side of things that has traditionally been science's purview. Creative Systems Theory argues for the importance of a more explicitly systemic science, and systemic not just in the sense of better including all the mechanistically related pieces (like a car is a system), but systemic in the creative sense that acknowledges deep connectedness as much as it does difference and distinction. The best of theorists in even the hardest of the sciences today view a narrowly right-hand, conceptual picture as simplistic and out of date. It is a recognition we will come back to with this chapter's third "ultimate question." For now, it is enough to note that a recognition of systemic interconnections has more and more come to shape the cutting edge of scientific understanding over the last century, from the linking of matter and energy in physics, to ecological perspectives in biology, to psychology's bringing together of conscious with unconscious. This new picture promises an increasingly provocative and vital kind of science in times to come.

Spirituality/religion and its ways of knowing present us with two different sorts of questions. The first is most familiar: Does God—or however we think of ultimate spiritual/religious authority—exist? Culturally mature perspective is limited in what it can directly say with regard to this kind of question. It does observe that the question confronts us with a challenge similar to what I've described with the task of stepping beyond parental notions of authority. And it does something more that ties directly to Creative Systems Theory's evolutionary perspective. It suggests that the standard "Is God real" question is really the wrong question. A person reading about how the theory addresses spirituality and religion could conclude that I might be making an argument for atheism. But in fact I find atheism as a concept rather silly. This is not because CST answers the God question, rather because the question as framed, resting as it does on polarized assumptions, can lead only to endlessly circular debate. Evolutionary perspective helps us ask more useful questions. In the end, atheism as an argument fails because it leaves the evolutionary dimension out of understanding.

If I argued, indeed became obsessed with arguing, that the ancient Greeks were wrong for believing there were gods atop Olympus, or that tribal societies have been wrong for having animistic deities, you would appropriately conclude that I had missed the point. While these kinds of beliefs tend not to work today, in their time they gave expression to an important kind of need, and more deeply, an essential aspect of human sensibility. While the common claim of the atheist that the more modern idea of a monotheistic God with a capital "G" has resulted in harm as well as benefit is accurate, CST proposes that the larger portion of that harm, while it may have been done in the name of religion, has been a product of our past need for worlds of us-versus-them rather than religion per se. And while the atheist's observation that religion makes little sense rationally and can lead to some assertions that are really quite absurd similarly has merit, in the end it fails to get at what is important. Religion through time has given expression to essential aspects of being human, aspects that are just as important in our time, and arguably now more important than ever. CST proposes that religion as we have known it in modern times is best thought of not in terms of the rightness or wrongness of its assertions, but as one chapter in an evolving story.

The second sort of question that spiritual/religious experience and its ways of knowing present concerns the nature of that story, both how it has contributed through history and how that contribution may now be changing. As with science, we want to answer religion's Question of Referent. And we want to understand more about how it can be addressed in our time. With this second sort of question, Creative Systems Theory and the concept of Cultural Maturity have a great deal to tell us, and this book's reflections have made a solid beginning.

It is important first to appreciate that the simple notion that there is a Question of Referent to answer by itself challenges traditional assumptions. Conventionally, religious truth is God's word (or the word of Allah, the utterance of a polytheistic pantheon, the inclinations of a collection of animistic forces, or whatever) and that is that. No larger perspective is needed—or desired. Here I've framed religious experience's ultimate purpose creatively. CST proposes that we can think of our diverse interpretations of the spiritual dimension as time- and space-specific expressions of the far extreme of archetypally feminine, left-hand sensibility as it manifests at a cultural scale.

We must be careful with such reframing to not just psychologize the sacred, a negation of the spiritual of which the social sciences have often rightfully been accused. The spiritual as understood in Creative Systems Theory's interpretation represents more than just projection from within ourselves (though the images we attach to our beliefs may be just that). Rather, it marks our felt connection with every aspect of creative context—the personal, interpersonal, and cultural, certainly; and, at least metaphorically, also the biological, and the cosmos as a whole.

To fully make sense of how a creative interpretation helps us look toward religion's future, we need to appreciate a quandary that the historical picture I've documented in this book presents for the spiritual dimension. I've described how the influence of right-hand sensibilities has increased over the course of history while that of left-hand sensibilities has gradually diminished. CST predicts that the influence of ways of thinking that draw at all deeply on the archetypally feminine would become largely eclipsed in our time, part of what I have described with the Dilemma of Trajectory. The Dilemma of Trajectory presents religion with a circumstance shared with other more left-hand social functions such as art and philosophy's more metaphysical aspects. It might seem to suggest that spiritual/religious experience has run its course.

Certainly if this direction were to continue unmodified, it would not bode well for things spiritual. We would appropriately pronounce God dead. Respected thinkers through the last century and earlier have argued just that, and not just thinkers from science, but also those of a more philosophical sort. Noting religion's role in world conflict, Bertrand Russell argued good riddance to any notion of divine causation: "[If life has] deliberate purpose, the purpose must have been that of a fiend. For my part, I find accident a less painful and more plausible hypothesis."[4]

The essential recognition for religion's future is that Integrative Metaperspective suggests a different result going forward. It affirms that the underlying sensibilities of religious/spiritual experience are pivotal in who we are—they can't really be lost. And it proposes that such sensibilities should not only continue to be important in the future, that importance should increase. I've described spiritual/religious experience in terms of four connectedness-related themes. Without them manifesting in some form in times to come, the likelihood that the species will make wise choices going forward becomes very small. We will need to expand how we hold these themes—for example, our connections in community must manifest as a new and deeper appreciation not just for people similar to ourselves, but also for our shared humanity—but we need what each theme describes if our future is to be healthy, and perhaps simply survivable. For people who identify strongly with religious belief, this picture presents reason to celebrate. If the concept of Cultural Maturity accurately describes today's fundamental task, in the future the sacred could manifest with even greater significance than in times past.

That said, the challenge that the concept of Cultural Maturity presents to religion is just as fundamental as that which it makes to science,

---

4 Bertrand Russell, *Why I Am Not a Christian*, George Allan & Unwin, 1927.

and for religion's advocates potentially even more disorienting. The price for a possible renewal will be high—extremely so. The doorway to this deepened spirituality can open only to the degree we are willing to reexamine much in the very foundations of belief.

Certainly the concept of Cultural Maturity brings into question culturally specific notions of the sacred. It argues that life in the future will be most unhappy if we cannot transcend differences of belief. This is especially the case where beliefs make one religion true and all others false (as through history they almost always have). Such beliefs are not compatible with life in a globally interconnected world.

Religion also comes up against Cultural Maturity's challenge to truth's past parental/mythologized status. Inherently that challenge includes spiritual truth. Whether manifest in the more maternal imagery of animism and mysticism or in the sterner and more philosophical images of patriarchal religious structures, the incarnate forms of sacred authority have served as mythic protectors, shielding us like children from the all-too-easily-overwhelming complexities and ambiguities of mortal life. Cultural Maturity's changes call into question the value of this kind of protection. Integrative Meta-perspective repeats the Reformation's call for responsibility in a further, quite ultimate way.

Both the Parts Work example and our box-of-crayons metaphor point toward a further kind of dislocation that many people will find even more disturbing. Culturally mature systemic perspective challenges the notion that spirituality lies at truth's center. It similarly does so for scientific truth and the truths of any other approach to knowing, but for many people, the fact that it might for religion can feel particularly disruptive. Integrative Meta-Perspective makes spiritual experience an important aspect of truth, but only that, an aspect. If we make the spiritual some last word today, it not only fails as truth we can rely on, ultimately it fails as spiritual truth—which to be the real thing must honor the particular truth challenges of its time. It is a realization that challenges new more "enlightened" notions of spiritual realization as much as it does traditional belief.

For our time, CST predicts for religion something very similar to what we witness today—an often conflicting mixture of doubt, dogmatism, and fresh, if often misguided, curiosity. Rarely is the result wholly satisfying. Many people find themselves deeply questioning religion, at least as conventionally conceived. Some of their concerns are fairly immediate—for example, sexual and financial transgressions of church leadership—but their doubts can also be more basic. Other people find reassurance in a regressive return to absolutist beliefs. The fact that past beliefs are being questioned can be interpreted as evidence that we need to adhere to them ever more strongly. And others still turn to New Age beliefs that are in fact not new at all.

Culturally mature perspective can't tell us just what spirituality in times ahead will look like. What it does say is that whatever we find, it should require that we think about the role of connectedness in ways that are fundamentally new—more complex and more complete. It also counsels us that connectedness is not the end of things and alerts us to numerous traps that come with believing that it might be. Culturally mature perspective's more whole-box-of-crayons picture challenges us to understand the sacred in ways that are more fully systemic, and systemic in ways not conceivable from within the worldviews of times past.[5]

An Expanded Picture

A person could imagine that because this more systemic interpretation requires us to step beyond thinking of either science or religion

---

5 We can in fact say a bit more about what getting there asks of us—which is a good thing given that the previous paragraph might suggest something terribly complicated. As tends to be the case with Cultural Maturity–related changes, we can think of the task as at once more radical and more ordinary than what we have known. Framing the task in terms of receptivity makes at least a good place to start. The simple act of being receptive helps us access the archetypally feminine. Going forward, we need to better engage experiences of all sorts more receptively and deeply—in our relationships with friends, when in nature, in self-reflection, in how we relate to our own bodies, in how we meet the larger world around us. Receptivity opens us to all of experience, but in particular it provides a direct doorway to the experience of connectedness. (Prayer and meditation still work too. Think of them as practical ways to engage deeply and receptively.) This simple task is of no small significance given the Dilemma of Trajectory. So much of life today is lived on the surface—from consumerism, to pop culture, to social media. To become a spiritual person in any deep sense in our time becomes a radical act. If the concept of Cultural Maturity is correct, it also inherently takes us into new territories of experience.

as final truths, it would leave our experience of these historically exalted realms diminished. But as we've seen with what happens when we move beyond other dynamics that have been thought of historically in polar terms, in fact it does the opposite. In times ahead, we should find ourselves better able not just to understand science and spirituality as aspects of a larger story, but also to better appreciate the profound contributions that each has made historically to that story. And we should come to think about both science and religion with a sophistication and nuance that has not before been an option.

The "Big Band Theory"—Creative Systems Theory Takes On Existence As a Whole

Can Creative Systems Theory help us better think about the whole shebang, existence in its entirety? Here it might not seem terribly pertinent. The theory's contribution lies with the human dimension, with who we are and how we understand. But in fact that is just what makes it relevant. Understanding our conclusions about existence as a whole necessarily starts with understanding the cognitive lenses through which we make sense of things.

We can't in the end know for sure what is "out there." Indeed, as philosophers are quick to tell us, we can't even be sure that there is an "out there" to know. But there is a lot we can say about understanding and understanding's evolution. CST addresses why through history we have thought not just about ourselves, but also about the physical and the biological, in the specific ways that we have. And of particular importance for these reflections, it proposes that there is a lot we can say about how today such understanding is changing.

Why did Newton and Descartes see a clockworks universe? And why, before that, did people in the Middle Ages see a universe ordered by religious/moral principles? What they understood reflected how they understood. And today that evolution continues. Whatever the scale of our concern, neither a clockworks picture nor its romantic or idealist complement are proving sufficient. Creative Systems Theory helps us make sense of why, what may lie ahead, and also why the world as we are beginning to see it has the characteristics that it does.

I've described how Cultural Maturity's cognitive reordering brings a more encompassing and complete vantage to how we think that

replaces Age of Reason formulations, in which truth reduced to rationality and simple cause-and-effect relationships, with ways of understanding that are more systemic and also more dynamic. This applies
to understandings of every sort. The world as we then see it is more
complexly interwoven and often more contradictory-seeming than
what we have known. It is also a world in which change, and often
change of a generative/evolutionary sort, becomes inherent to how
things work, and in which uncertainty plays a newly key role. We
could say that Integrative Meta-perspective offers entry into a world
that is more explicitly creative.

When we apply the word "creative" to existence as a whole we need
to take particular care. We've tended historically to project how we
have thought onto everything around us—to in effect see the world in
our own image. We witnessed this with how the Age of Reason's ratio-
nalistic lens gave us a machine model world. If we are not careful, we
can fall prey to a related trap and make the whole of existence creative
in the specific sense that we as humans are creative. But fortunately,
culturally mature perspective and a creative frame can provide help
here too. The stepping back that comes with Integrative Meta-perspective's overarching vantage helps us better distinguish ourselves from
what we wish to understand. And Creative Systems Theory helps us
better appreciate not just the rich interconnections and often provocative generativities of existence as a whole, but also essential differences
in how it is that various aspects of existence may be creative.

Just for fun, we could call the encompassing picture that results the
"Big Band Theory" of existence. I don't consider it a formal part of
Creative Systems Theory—indeed, not a theory at all in the traditional
sense. It is more a metaphor that follows from CST's conclusions, a
thought experiment that invites us to reflect on what existence as a
whole might look like when viewed through a creative lens.

Polarity, Integrative Meta-perspective, and a Creative Frame

A small handful of polarity-related observations provide a start with
this big-picture reframing task. The first relates to how it has been our
tendency in times past to divide not just particular beliefs, but also
the entirety of existence, into polar worlds. We've done this in different ways depending on when in history we look. We've also done it

in different ways depending on whether our basic inclinations have tended more toward the material/scientific or spiritual/religious side of things. In modern times, science has divided existence into animate and inanimate, lumping ourselves together with the creaturely and setting this in contrast to a "dead" world of rocks and rivers. Religion has tended more to place the human species separate, make us in some way "chosen" with dominion over the rest of creation. With Cultural Maturity's cognitive changes, we would expect that we might begin to think about existence in its entirety more as a whole. It is something we are beginning to see.

A second overarching polarity-related observation concerns change and just how it happens. Past explanations with regard to change have also been polar. They've posited some separate driving impetus, be it in earliest times an animistic force, or with modern, more mechanistic thinking, an action with its equal and opposite reaction. Ideas about change too are changing. Increasingly we find thinking that makes change and stability aspects of larger ways of understanding. Dualistic formulations—both of the extreme type that posits a distinct animating presence and of the more mundane sort that juxtaposes separate causes and effects—are giving way to more dynamic ways of thinking. And often, "dynamic" refers not just to having more moving parts, but to being somehow generative. Change and the coherence through which we identify something as having existence become parts of a single larger, "self-organizing" picture.

These two polarity-related observations taken together help bring a more systemically conceived picture into focus. When we leave behind thinking of existence as a whole in polar terms, we find ourselves newly interested in complex interconnections, the necessary role of uncertainty, and more encompassing ways of understanding the big picture. And when we similarly think about change more systemically, we better appreciate how stability as we think of it is ultimately dependent on the fact of change and how change works in ways that are more dynamic and creative than before we have assumed.

For this new picture to be complete, we also need a third kind of recognition. It concerns the unique ways that various layers/levels of existence give this more systemic picture expression. I've emphasized how culturally mature perspective, along with alerting us to interconnections, also brings a deeper understanding of real difference. When we fall for ideology, this sort of difference can be one of the first things that gets lost. Classical science can reduce it all to mechanistic physics. And various Unity Fallacy formulations can make big-picture interpretation but another way of arguing that "all is one." A creative frame suggests that the basic recognition that differences are always as important as similarities should apply to different aspects of existence as a whole.

It suffices for our purposes to keep things simple and talk in terms of the three levels that everyday thought suggests: there is inanimate creation; there is life; and there is this odd addition, conscious life (including ourselves and to lesser degrees other higher life forms). Seen from the vantage of culturally mature perspective, these layers/levels become unique manifestations of existence's creative dynamism. I find a familiar image useful: Neapolitan ice cream. Each layer/level is at once the same stuff (like ice cream) and wholly different. Actually, what we then see somewhat stretches the ice cream metaphor. The various layers/levels, rather than being just different in kind (as with flavors), reflect distinct levels of organization. The systems concept of "emergent properties" helps us complete the needed stretch. Emergent properties are characteristics unique to a set of systemic relationships. In the new picture, each level is defined/separated/joined by an emergent property—in this case existence (in contrast to non-existence), life, and the capacity for conscious reflection.

A creative frame also lets us be more specific. Instead of ice cream, the "same stuff" becomes creation (in the most encompassing sense). And what differentiates these various emergent realities is the amount of complexity and agency—we could say creative information—each reflects. Each new layer/level is distinguished by a "creative multiplier" (or several creative multipliers working together) that radically increases the rate at which creative reorganization can take place. In the case of life, the creative multipliers are genetic coding, new adaptive capacities, and natural selection. In the case of ourselves, the multiplier is the option of fresh creation happening with every new "aha" that arises with conscious awareness and our unique toolmaking, idea-making, meaning-making prowess. The innovations that separate the various layers/levels of existence qualitatively increase the amount of creation/formativeness each succeeding layer/level is capable of manifesting. In this way, the application of a creative frame helps us both appreciate interconnectedness and grasp how layers/levels are fundamentally different from one another.

Let's look briefly at the various layers of this new kind of picture as seen specifically through the lens of science. With scientific understanding over the last century (and even before), we have witnessed the beginnings of a specifically more creative kind of interpretation. We've found interconnectedness more deeply appreciated, change manifesting as an intrinsic attribute of each systemic level's functioning, and uncertainty playing a newly integral role. We've also seen insights about the transitions that at once link and separate the various aspects of this more systemic picture.[6]

The physical: It is with the hard sciences that people are most likely to recognize that we are witnessing something new, and new in a radical sense. Albert Einstein's special relativity provocatively linked the before separate worlds of time and space. Later, general relativity provided a more systemic approach to understanding gravity, a phenomenon that always before had been thought of as distinct and mysterious. Both formulations left mechanistic/deterministic thinking intact, but Einstein's physics colleagues, and ultimately the general public, also rightly came to view these contributions as revolutionary. The early thinking of quantum mechanics, the work of Niels Bohr and colleagues, presented a more direct challenge, throwing understanding into a world that directly confronted deterministic assumptions. Waves

---

6   The general direction of these observations is not original to me. The recognition that we can understand reality as a whole in more encompassing ways is in some form increasingly common. But popular interpretations tend to either remain mechanistic or reduce to Unity Fallacy thinking. (Some Unity Fallacy views can go so far as to conclude that existence as a whole is intelligent or in some way alive or conscious.) We find a giveaway for Unity Fallacy conclusions noted earlier in how such views often make analogy with the thinking of early stages in culture. I emphasize again that while an appreciation for connectedness stood at the center of early thought—and in an important sense needs to be remembered (that concept of Reengagement)—the kind of thinking needed for going forward is new to our time.

and particles, energy and matter suddenly became less "things" than alternative kinds of observations. In quantum mechanics, the answer to the question of which is most real depends on when and how you look.

Contributions at the biggest of cosmic scales would prove similarly radical. Edwin Hubble's demonstration that the universe is expanding required that science abandon its previous picture of a stable, eternally constant cosmos. The Big Bang Theory—the idea that the universe in fact had a beginning, and a dramatic one—followed from these essential observations. Today, insights from our study of the heavens reveal an ever more dramatically shape-shifting world of quasars, pulsars, white dwarfs, and black holes. Black holes, in particular, point toward a more generative interpretation. In the new picture, creation, rather than being either established by a separate entity or something that has always existed, becomes a process inherent to the larger story of existence.

A further pertinent contribution from physics, the phenomenon known as "entanglement," has gotten particular attention of late. It turns out that subatomic particles that are linked by virtue of being complementary can remain linked even when separated by significant distances. The connection is not causal in a traditional sense. And it is immediate—not limited by the speed of light. While entanglement was originally assumed to require proximity, recent experiments done between an orbiting satellite and the earth suggest that distance is not an obstacle. Entangled links are fragile and easily disrupted, but the phenomenon of entanglement has rich potential applications in both communication and computing. It also raises fascinating questions about the nature of connectedness in the universe and just how connected things may be.[7]

---

7 Questions about what might allow transition from one layer to another take on special importance with interpretations that view existence as at once continuous and discontinuous. With the transition from the inanimate to life, I think immediately of the contribution of Nobel chemist Ilya Prigogine. Prigogine demonstrated how certain non-living systems under the right conditions could self-maintain and self-organize, work that contributed to a growing consensus among scientists that the emergent property we call life, rather than some rare, perhaps one-off chance occurrence, may be, if not almost inevitable, certainly more readily achieved than we

Life: Arguably biology's newly "creative" picture began even earlier—with Charles Darwin's publication of *Origins of Species* and Gregor Mendel's later work with pea plants that demonstrated the actions of "invisible factors" that we now call genes. Evolutionary biology presents a picture of life in which creation, rather than something that happens to life, is understood as following in an ongoing way from the nature of life. Ecological thought, first formally introduced with explorations of food webs and food cycles in the 1920s, added important further pieces to biology's new, more systemic picture. Today it is so familiar to us that we can miss its radical significance. Both interconnectedness and change are intrinsic to ecological thought. Increasingly it has become second nature for biologists to think in terms of communities and ecosystems and the interplaying life cycles of organisms and populations.

Neither of these contributions in biology—at least in their early forms—fundamentally challenged mechanistic assumptions (the best of thinking today in both evolutionary and systems biology begins to do so). But new attention brought by biologists to the age-old "what is life" quandary confronted the classical picture directly. Historically, the life question has been answered in two primary ways. I've described how modern scientists have tended to think of life as just a very complex machine. Looking back, we are more likely to find explanations that locate life's source in some separate animating force—from Aristotle's early more dualistic formulations; to, in medieval times, a separate religiously defined soul that directs action; to, with nineteenth-century vitalism, a distinct animating energy.

With the middle of the last century, early systems thinkers challenged both views and argued that we needed to understand living systems as integrated wholes. Previously I noted the contribution of Ludwig von Bertalanffy. His thinking emphasized the fact that living

---

have before assumed. Prigogine and I were in conversation during the time of the writing of my first book. (See Ilya Prigogine, *From Being to Becoming,* W.H Freeman, 1980.) We can think of ideas from the mathematics of complexity as at least relevant here. Complexity theory demonstrates how immensely complex dynamics can be products of very simple equations. With the mathematics of complexity we remain very specifically within mechanistic models, but the generation of complexity is clearly pertinent to what is needed for life.

systems are open systems, systems that maintain themselves in highly dynamic states far from equilibrium. Somewhat later we saw attention given to feedback loops and self-regulation. The work of biologist and systems theorist Gregory Bateson—who argued that if we understood understanding deeply, we will have understood life—has particular pertinence.[8]

Recent contributions from biology have added a further important cognition-related insight. Organizational mechanisms have traditionally been framed in command-and-control terms. Brains ran bodies; DNA ran cells. We are better recognizing how cells, tissues, and organs of more complex organisms often engage their worlds through complexly networked and often highly decentralized informational processes.

Biology also provides other pertinent new insights. It is recognizing, for example, how creatures of all sorts are more complex, and complexly intelligent, than we have before assumed. Increasingly the important question with regard to intelligence has become not how intelligent a creature might be, but just how it is intelligent. Biology is also better appreciating how evolution is as much about cooperation as competition, and not just cooperation with one's own kind, but also between species (think of the increasingly recognized role of bacteria in our gut—they keep us healthy and we in turn keep them nourished and alive). Of particular significance, the question of what it means to think about living systems in living terms is being acknowledged more and more by biologists not just as legitimate, but as pivotal to effective understanding.[9]

---

8 See Gregory Bateson, *Mind and Nature: A Necessary Unity*, Bantam, 1980.

9 With transitional dynamics between life and conscious life, at the least we are recognizing that the boundary is less clear-cut than we have assumed. Even the most humble paramecium or ameba, it turns out, is conscious in the sense of actively responding to the world around it. And higher life forms, certainly birds and other mammals, are at least somewhat conscious in the more specific sense we have historically reserved for ourselves. We are left with the question—today increasingly legitimate to ask—of whether conscious awareness in the human sense might best be thought of as an almost inevitable consequence of life. Previous reflections in this chapter on free will and determinism invite us to come at this interface more from

Human Life: I've observed how we find precursors of a more dynamic and systemic picture for the human sphere in the best of early thinking in psychiatry and psychology. The radical recognition that much that is most important in being human functions out of conscious awareness provided initial insights. And I've noted how we can think of the first decades of modern psychiatry and psychology's evolution as an inquiry into intelligence's multiple ways of knowing. In the middle part of the last century, we also saw efforts to bring formal systems thinking into psychology, particularly with family therapy and work with organizations, but also with studies of perception. Such efforts today are further supported by technical innovations such as advanced imaging techniques. One increasingly recognized conclusion is particularly pertinent to this more systemically complex, self-organizing picture. It appears that conscious awareness, rather than being located in some particular part of the brain, is best thought of as an emergent capacity of our neurology as a whole.

Creative Systems Theory makes its specific contribution at this level of creative organization. I've described how the theory's framing of understanding in the human sphere begins with an explicitly creative assertion, that what makes us unusual as creatures is our striking creative proclivities. We've seen how human intelligence is structured specifically to support and drive creative/formative process. And we've looked too at how we can understand all manner of phenomena—such as the human experience of meaning, the ways human developmental processes progress, and how it is that different people think and act as differently as they do—in terms of patterns that follow from the ultimately creative nature of human cognition.

Our Place in the Scheme of Things

A creative frame invites conjecture with regard to a related but more specific eternal question: What is our place in the larger scheme of things? We can put the question in science-versus-religion terms. From a scientific viewpoint, we might appropriately ask—as many great

---

the human side. Integrative Meta-perspective's more fully creative "bridging" of mind and body suggests a more intimately systemic relationship with the creaturely in ourselves than before we have acknowledged.

thinkers have asked—"Are we but a speck in an essentially purposeless universe, an odd momentary impulse of no real ultimate significance?" Or do we better think of ourselves as God's special children, as most religions through time have in some way seen us? A creative perspective provides a third option—neither quite so random nor quite so grand, but arguably more intriguing.

Our place in the larger scheme of things? At the least we represent a fascinating bit of creative innovation (with the jury far from in on just how ultimately successful). If we want to feel a bit more special, we could claim ours to be a particularly significant sort of creative innovation. We are the only creature, at least on our particular earth, that is not just consciously aware, but aware of itself as part of something that has evolved and continues to evolve. In an interesting sense, through us, creation, not just as fact but as process, has become conscious of itself.

In a way, this interpretation makes our human achievement even more remarkable. But it also makes it more tenuous, more explicitly "experimental." It is quite possible that exactly that which makes us special—our great creative prowess—will be our undoing. Our time on the planet has been extremely short (compared to, say, the dinosaurs—for us 300,000 years with civilization a product of only the most recent 20,000, compared to 180 million years for the dinosaurs). And with growing frequency, modern invention, and human choice more generally, has dangerously two-edged potential consequences. In our time, the human creative experiment continues, and in ways that have major implications for its ultimate success.

Cultural Maturity's cognitive changes make this more fully creative kind of big-picture interpretation possible. They also have a critical role with regard to where it all might lead. Integrative Meta-perspective describes the possibility—and necessity—of a more aware and more deeply engaged relationship with our creative, toolmaking, meaning-making natures. Homo sapiens sapiens—"man the wise"—is perhaps coming to better deserve his audaciously proclaimed status (proclaimed twice over for emphasis). If Creative Systems Theory is correct, certainly our continued well-being, and perhaps our survival, depends on it.

Stumbling Awkwardly Toward the Possible

My purpose with this short book has been to bring clarity to the leap in understanding that Creative Systems Theory and the concept of Cultural Maturity represent. I've attempted to highlight that leap's significance, both its practical significance and its larger significance in the history of ideas. And I've endeavored to delineate just how CST and the concept of Cultural Maturity succeed in making it. I've argued that while my claims might seem audacious, this is only because of the fundamental way in which these ideas stretch how we usually think. I've proposed that in the end these notions represent common sense, simply a maturity of common sense that we are not accustomed to. If I am right, they are audacious in a way that is critical if we are to continue to advance as a species.

We can briefly summarize both the audaciousness and the contribution with a couple of simple questions. The first question: *Just how are Creative Systems Theory and the concept of Cultural Maturity different from what we have known?* I've described how they reflect reality as viewed from the vantage of Integrative Meta-perspective, when we at once more fully step back from and more deeply engage the whole of our cognitive complexity. As such, Creative Systems Theory and the concept of Cultural Maturity are different in being more complete than what we have known. They better give expression to the whole of who we are and how we understand. They also offer a newly dynamic and systemic way of making sense of ourselves and our worlds, one that is more consistent with the fact that we are alive and human. Developmentally, they represent a next essential stage in how we think and act.

And the second question: *Just what makes such differences important?* I've described how Creative Systems Theory and the concept of Cultural Maturity provide ways of understanding that will be increasingly important going forward. The concept of Cultural Maturity offers a new guiding narrative and highlights new skills and capacities that will be essential if we are to effectively engage critical challenges before us. I've argued that if the concept of Cultural Maturity is not basically correct, it is hard to be legitimately optimistic about our human future. Creative Systems Theory brings detail to culturally mature perspective. The theory's application of a creative frame invites us to understand with a newly possible—and newly critical—kind of sophistication and nuance. It also helps separate the wheat from the chaff in our thinking as we attempt to go forward.

New Concepts and Insights

We can be more specific about what is new by summarizing the major concepts I've introduced in the book. These include:

1) The concept of Cultural Maturity as understood in relationship to Integrative Meta-perspective's cognitive reordering.

2) The Dilemma of Differentiation and its relationship to the challenge of thinking in ways that reflect that we are living, human beings.

3) The application of a creative frame as a solution to the problem of understanding in living systems terms and as a way to bring detail and nuance to understanding in human systems.

4) A creative framing of polarity and its relationship to developmental processes.

5) A creative framing of intelligence's multiplicity.

6) The Myth of the Individual and a more systemic understanding of both identity and human relationship.

7) With the idea of Whole-Person/Whole-System patterning concepts, how Integrative Meta-perspective makes it possible to think about truth at its most basic in ways that get beyond ideological assumptions.

8) Patterning in Time concepts that let us address temporal context.

9) Patterning in Space concepts that provide a way to address here-and-now contextual variables.

10) Parts Work as a major contribution to available approaches for inquiry and understanding.

A Few More Specific Questions

A handful of more specific questions help fill out where these notions take us and the consequences—both consequences that may at first be unsettling and those that we should clearly celebrate:

▦ *What do we necessarily leave behind with culturally mature understanding?* Integrative Meta-perspective requires that we surrender much that in times past has been essential to our experience of purpose and identity. Depending on our Capacitance, we may experience these losses as threats or invitations to step forward. Cultural Maturity's cognitive reordering takes us beyond:

- "Chosen-people" notions of national and social identity.
- Heroic and romantic concepts of limitless possibility.
- The idea that truths are fixed and absolute.
- Mythologized notions of leadership.
- Absolutist moral codes.
- The equating of rationality with intelligence.
- The idea that one person can be the answer and completion for another.
- A belief in identity as who we think we are and unfettered free will as an expression of such identity.
- Postmodern beliefs that make truth's options endless.
- Parental/omniscient notions of spiritual truth.
- Mechanistic/deterministic science as a last word.

▦ *How does culturally mature perspective alter how we think and act?* We come back to the new skills and capacities that come with Cultural Maturity's changes. These new abilities are necessary if letting go of past absolutist ways of understanding is not to just throw us into chaos. Integrative Meta-perspective brings with it:

- The greater responsibility needed if we no longer relate to culture as a symbolic parent.
- Greater tolerance for uncertainty and complexity.
- An acceptance of the fact of real limits.
- The ability to step beyond ideological assumptions, both those

that we hold collectively as a product of our time in culture and those that reflect more particular ideological beliefs.

- The ability to hold polarity—and multiplicity more generally—systemically.
- The capacity to draw consciously on intelligence's multiple aspects.
- An appreciation for how truth is contextual—relative to its time and to the larger systemic relationships of which it is a part.

What more specific new possibilities follow from Cultural Maturity's cognitive changes? With Cultural Maturity's cognitive reordering we find fundamental changes in how we see ourselves and our worlds and also in how we make choices. Integrative Meta-perspective makes possible:

- The ability to bring a newly overarching kind of big-picture, long-term perspective to our considerations.
- A world in which the us-versus-them dynamics that have traditionally led to war and defined relationships between social groups play much less of a role.
- A significant lessening of ideological polarization with a greater capacity both for collaboration and for addressing questions systemically.
- In making choices, the ability to better assess risk and appreciate creative options.
- With the deepened recognition of intelligence's rich complexity, a more complete and potential-filled understanding of both identity and truth.
- The possibility of interpersonal relationships of all sorts that better reflect connections between whole people.
- A significant lessening of bigotry of all sorts, and at once a greater appreciation of real differences.
- The ability to live our personal and collective lives from values that better reflect the whole of what is important to us.
- A deeper and more multifaceted kind of spirituality, and at once, a more dynamic and complete kind of science.
- A deepened appreciation for our responsibility in nature and for making sustainable and ultimately life-affirming choices on the planet.

▨ *And what does Creative Systems Theory add to this basic expansion of worldview?* Creative Systems Theory adds to these achievements the application of a creative frame and the conceptual detail that becomes possible with the theory's various patterning concepts. In doing so, it provides essential nuance. It also further highlights both how culturally mature perspective take us beyond past ways of understanding and the importance of doing so:

- CST's developmental framework provides some of the best evidence for why we might predict the kind of "growing up" as a species that the concept of Cultural Maturity describes. It also provides explanation for how it is that Cultural Maturity involves changes not just in what we think, but in how we think—specific cognitive changes. And it helps us understand the particular form that this cognitive reordering takes.
- By offering a framework for addressing concerns of all sorts more systemically, the theory brings detail to what good decision-making in all parts of our personal and collective lives will require of us. Its various patterning concepts provide conceptual tools for getting beyond the simple-answer, ideological conclusions of times past. They also help make visible the more demanding questions that ideological beliefs have protected us from recognizing.
- By deepening and bringing detail to our understanding of human intelligence, CST helps us better grasp the multifaceted nature of understanding. It also brings attention to how the various aspects of human intelligence work together to give us our amazing innovative capacities. The whole of CST can be understood to follow from this creative framing of intelligence's mechanisms.
- With the radical observation that change in human systems organizes creatively, the theory makes it possible to understand human developmental processes of all sorts—from individual psychological development, to the growth of relationships, to the evolution of social systems at the largest of scales—in more dynamic, nuanced, and integrated ways.
- CST patterning concepts help us better understand history—and not just the facts of history, but the evolution of beliefs, institutional forms, and our felt experience of meaning. They help us

better grasp the human story as a story—one with chapters, and one with possible chapters yet to come. They help us rethink the past, and also better understand current challenges and the tasks ahead for the species.

- CST patterning concepts highlight and bring detail to how understanding always happens in a context. This includes change-related contexts, what we find with an appreciation for developmental dynamics, and also more here-and-now contextual relativities. All of CST's patterning concepts are in some way about bringing greater nuance to our appreciation of context.

- CST's creative frame combined with its various patterning concepts help us address a wide array of truth-related concerns where the thinking of times past is today proving inadequate. For example, they help us understand morality, relationships of all sorts, and the dynamics of identity in more complete—dynamic and systemic—ways. They also help us rethink whole domains of understanding—education, medicine, governance, religion, science, and more.

- The theory includes a nuanced set of tools for identifying traps in our thinking, both in our personal understandings and more collectively, including when it comes to thinking about the future. Besides helping us appreciate how the more obvious of ideological beliefs fail us, the theory also helps us grasp how postmodern thinking or ideas that view the future only in terms of new technologies are in the end just as ideological, and how today they often put us in particular danger.

- CST's creative framing of intelligence and truth helps us address many eternal quandaries—from the nature of conscious awareness to how the relationship between the spiritual and material might best be understood—ultimate questions that have always before left us baffled. The theory proposes that the reason the answers to such questions have before eluded us is that Integrative Meta-perspective is needed to ask them in ultimately useful ways. A creative frame can make answers not just possible but often, with reflection, almost obvious.

- Specific CST concepts such as our time's Crisis of Purpose, the Dilemma of Trajectory, and Transitional Absurdity help make troubling and easily confusing current circumstances more understandable.

- CST provides not just ideas, but also methodologies. It includes an array of specific "hands-on" approaches that actively support the kind of understanding on which our future depends.

Where We Stand

I've noted that only about 5 percent of the population in the modern West is currently capable of significantly developed culturally mature understanding. Given my claim that unless the concept of Cultural Maturity is basically correct it is hard to be hopeful about our human future, this number might legitimately evoke concern. But the situation may not be as dire as it could seem. In part this is because effective leadership doesn't necessarily require as much realization on the part of leaders as we tend to imagine. Effective leadership needs to be at least a bit ahead of its time, but it can't be too far ahead. There is also how, if Creative Systems Theory is correct, we don't have to create the new, more mature ways of understanding from whole cloth. I've described how at least the potential for needed changes is developmentally built into who we are. In addition, there is how change in human systems, even fundamental change, can happen more quickly than we might imagine. Historically, major cultural change has tended to happen in leaps.

That said, with decades now behind me training leaders, I do have significant concern. I've described how addressing any of the most critical challenges before us will require culturally mature capacities. And I've observed that we have often witnessed regression with regard to these capacities in recent decades. While cultural change often happens in a two-steps-forward-one-step-back fashion, such regression is not something I would necessarily have predicted. I am very careful not to make observations that only fuel cynicism—cynicism is too easy and has no purpose. But it also appears quite possible that generations immediately ahead will face realities that are more demanding—and perhaps often brutish—than I might have previously suggested.

A major reason that I've written this book and others is that I believe foresight provides the most effective way forward. I hope that I've been able to communicate how ways forward are very real—indeed, predicted—if we can bring the needed awareness and courage to bear. I hope, too, that I've been able to make clear how possibilities before us are in potential not just significant, but profound.

INDEX

ICD Press is the publishing arm of the Institute for Creative Development. Information about the Institute and other Institute publications can be found on Charles Johnston's Author Page www.CharlesJohnstonmd.com

The Institute for Creative Development (ICD) Press
4324 Meridian Ave. N.
Seattle WA 98103
206-526-8562